READING with PICTURES

VOLUME ONE

Cover Illustration by:
Jill Thompson

A SPECIAL THANKS

To our contributors, editors and other volunteers: Together we've taken the first step on an incredible journey, a journey made possible by your hard work and dedication.

To our donors and pre-order backers: We literally could not have done this without you.

To our allies in education, academia and the comics community: We stand on the shoulders of giants, and we're honored to join you in the larger movement to serve students everywhere by expanding the definition of literacy itself.

www.readingwithpictures.org
Getting comics into schools and getting schools into comics.

Josh Elder - Publisher and Editor-in-Chief
Rob Valois - Managing Editor
Brandon Montclare - Editor
Sari Wilson - Editor
Camilla Zhang - Associate Editor

Reading With Pictures

EXECUTIVE DIRECTOR:
Josh Elder

BOARD OF DIRECTORS:
Katie Doland
Michael Moreci
Trevor Mueller
David Rapp
Tim Sarrantonio
John Shableski
Rob Valois

Table of Contents

Foreword

Open any children's book–Eric Carle, Dr. Seuss, take your pick–and you'll experience rich visual imagery combined with literary text. We present these books to young children, knowing that they will adore the pictures, engage in the narratives, seek more books, eventually learn to read, and hopefully love to read. Yet as children get older and enter school systems, the pictures quickly fall by the wayside. We expect students to become "serious" readers, working toward paragraph-based chapter books and the accepted canon of classic literature. For those students, like me, who loved to read at an early age, this entrenched method was a non-issue. For countless others, however, reading was, and still is, a struggle and seemingly insurmountable barrier to success in school.

This book and the organization behind it–Reading With Pictures–aims to turn the reading paradigm on its head through the medium of comics. With their mission of "Getting Comics into Schools and Schools into Comics," Reading With Pictures is helping teachers foster a love of reading through the natural marriage of words and pictures that is comics. You need not be a comics enthusiast to appreciate and utilize the pages that follow here. Rather, all you need is an open mind and willingness to do whatever it takes to help all children become accomplished, enthusiastic readers.

In fact, I wish I had this book in hand during my first teaching experience with an unwieldy class of 34 New York City fifth-graders. I clearly remember a group of four boys in the back of the room who ignored everything I said and opted instead to draw Pokemon characters. More out of frustration than anything, I told the boys that if they would write words in cartoon balloons next to their drawings, I could evaluate their writing and give them a grade. I liken that statement to the starting gun of a race: *BOOM!!* The boys were off creating comics–volume after volume of written, artistic narratives designed in class, during recess, after school, on the bus, and wherever else they could find a flat surface. It should come as no surprise that the boys' writing improved dramatically. They became dedicated readers of comics and other books, and they went on to achieve great things in school.

And for me, the seed was planted for the Comic Book Project (www.ComicBookProject.org), an initiative that I founded in 2001 to engage youths from high-poverty neighborhoods in the process of planning, writing, designing, and publishing original comic books. CBP has since grown to become an international model for literacy engagement and reinforcement, with tens of thousands of comic books created by students in grades K-12 from Florida to Hawaii, Mexico to Nigeria. The growth of CBP has been largely due to the partnerships that we have built with organizations and people who champion our cause of creativity as a crucial element of literacy learning.

One of those champions is Josh Elder, Executive Director of Reading With Pictures. I first met Josh in April, 2010, when the International Reading Association had unexpectedly canceled its Graphic Novel Institute—a telltale sign of the fragile relationship between comics and the reading establishment. With what seemed like truly superhuman power and speed, Josh rekindled the Institute by garnering the support of Northwestern University, Diamond Comics, First:Second Books, and a wealth of presenters and panelists, including comics creators, children's authors, and academic researchers.

Many wonderful things transpired at the Institute. Jane Yolen, the renowned children's book author, described her dedication to comics as made evident by her most recent book, a graphic novel titled *Foiled*. Bill Ayers, Professor of Education at University of Illinois at Chicago, donned a Boondocks t-shirt and presented the graphic novel version of his memoir *To Teach—The Journey in Comics*. But most exciting was the participation of school teachers and librarians who have embraced comics as literature and literacy reinforcement. These educators shared their successes in introducing comics into their classrooms and libraries, as well as the challenges they regularly face from principals, parents, and other teachers. All through these proceedings, Josh Elder guided the conversations and presentations. Thanks to him, everyone walked away from the Institute inspired and ready for more comics in our curricula.

Perhaps you are one of those educators excited about how comics can engage and motivate your students. Perhaps you are one of those skeptical principals or parents, unsure of why your children won't put down their beloved comic books and graphic novels. Or maybe you are just a bit curious about comics in education and the role that comics can play in the lives of young people. Regardless, this Anthology will be an invaluable resource for you. Enjoy it, and all the possibilities that it holds for readers of any age.

Dr. Michael Bitz, EdD
Founder of the Comic Book Project
Executive Director of the Center for Educational Pathways
www.edpath.org

..., BACK IN THE CAVEMAN DAYS THERE WAS NO WRITTEN LANGUAGE YET. SO THESE CAVE MEN AND CAVE WOMEN WOULD RECORD THEIR LIVES AND STORIES BY PAINTING ON CAVE WALLS!

G-MAN

Reign of the Robo-Teachers

story and art by Chris Giarrusso   chrisGcomics.com

CLASS, AS YOU ALL KNOW, THE SCHOOL DISTRICT VOTED TO SAVE MONEY BY REPLACING THE TEACHING STAFF WITH ROBOTS, AND SO TODAY I MUST SAY GOODBYE.

STARTING NOW, ALL OF THE OTHER SCHOOL TEACHERS IN THE DISTRICT AND I WILL BE TURNING YOU OVER TO THE NEW *ROBO-TEACHERS.*

THAT WILL BE ALL, MR. JASON W. GAVIN. YOU ARE DISMISSED.

I ALWAYS SAID THE INEVITABLE DAY WOULD COME WHEN ROBOTS WOULD REPLACE ALL HUMANS.

I'M REALLY GOING TO MISS EACH AND EVERY ONE OF--

EXIT THE CLASSROOM NOW, MR. GAVIN!

WOW, THIS IS *GREAT!*

I CAN'T BELIEVE WE'RE FINALLY FREE OF OL' MR. GAVIN ONCE AND FOR ALL!

ZZAPP!

THERE WILL BE NO SPEAKING OUT OF TURN, PERRY BECHETT!

ZZZAP!

GEH!

I GUESS MR. GAVIN WASN'T SO BAD AFTER--

THERE WILL BE NO SPEAKING OUT OF TURN, CHARLES HENAY!

ZZAPP!

IDIOT.

WHAT PART OF "NO SPEAKING" DIDN'T YOU UNDERST--

THERE WILL BE NO SPEAKING OUT OF TURN, LEE-ANNE WEBER!

ZZAPP!

LATER THAT DAY...

I'VE NEVER SEEN THE PLAYGROUND THIS EMPTY DURING RECESS!

EVERYONE'S GETTING ELECTROCUTED AND HOSPITALIZED!

AND ALSO GETTING THEIR RECESS TAKEN AWAY!

ZZZAPP!

NO RUNNING DURING RECESS. LIFE IS NOT A GAME.

THESE ROBO-TEACHERS ARE REALLY CRACKING DOWN!

IT'S THE SAME IN OUR CLASS.

NOT FOR LONG!

WHAT DOES *THAT* MEAN, COMPUTER JASON?

WHY DO YOU INSIST ON ALWAYS SPEAKING IN RIDDLES?

EXPLAIN YOURSELF IN A STRAIGHTFORWARD MANNER FOR ONCE!

I'M HACKING INTO THE ROBO-SYSTEM.

I THINK WE'LL FIND THESE ROBO-TEACHERS A LOT MORE *AGREEABLE* AFTER RECESS.

AND SO...

ATTENTION STUDENTS.

CLASS IS BACK IN SESSION.

PUT AWAY YOUR BOOKS AND START TALKING TO EACH OTHER.

ARE YOU *SERIOUS?* WE SHOULD *TALK?*

WE DON'T WANT TO GET ZAPPED FOR TALKING.

TALKING TO EACH OTHER IS TODAY'S LESSON. DISCUSS YOUR FAVORITE TOYS, VIDEO GAMES, AND TV SHOWS WITH EACH OTHER OR FAIL.

ALL RIGHT!

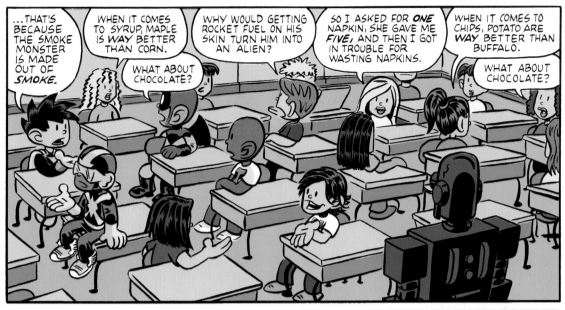

...THAT'S BECAUSE THE SMOKE MONSTER IS MADE OUT OF *SMOKE*.

WHEN IT COMES TO SYRUP, MAPLE IS *WAY* BETTER THAN CORN.

WHAT ABOUT CHOCOLATE?

WHY WOULD GETTING ROCKET FUEL ON HIS SKIN TURN HIM INTO AN ALIEN?

SO I ASKED FOR *ONE* NAPKIN, SHE GAVE ME *FIVE*, AND THEN I GOT IN TROUBLE FOR WASTING NAPKINS.

WHEN IT COMES TO CHIPS, POTATO ARE *WAY* BETTER THAN BUFFALO.

WHAT ABOUT CHOCOLATE?

THEY NEVER EVEN *ASKED* FOR THOSE ROCKS UNDER THE TREE!

ORANGE? I LIKE *GRAPE*.

YOU MISSED THE BEGINNING.

ZAP!

WHU--

WHAT WAS *THAT* FOR?

I WASN'T *DOING* ANYTHING!

YOUR ASSIGNMENT IS TO TALK.

SILENT DAY-DREAMING IS NOT AN OPTION, JACK HAYES.

FAIL.

ATTENTION, CLASS. YOUR HOMEWORK ASSIGNMENT IS AS FOLLOWS:

EAT A CANDY BAR FOR DINNER.

CANDY

CLASS DISMISSED.

SO...

...HOW WAS YOUR FIRST DAY WITH THE ROBO-TEACHERS?

IT WAS *CRAZY!* THE ROBO-TEACHERS KEPT ZAPPING KIDS FOR EVERY LITTLE THING THEY DID WRONG! WITH LASERS... OR TASERS... OR SOMETHING.

OH, *STOP IT,* MICHAEL. THEY *WERE NOT.*

A KID IN MY CLASS GOT ZAPPED FOR *SNEEZING.*

THE SCHOOL DISTRICT WOULD NOT PROGRAM THESE ROBO-TEACHERS TO *ZAP* YOU. THAT'S *ABSURD.*

IT WAS ONE OF THOSE THREE-SNEEZES-IN-A-ROW DEALS, SO HE GOT ZAPPED THREE TIMES.

HE'S IN THE HOSPITAL NOW.

STOP YOUR RIDICULOUS STORIES AND EAT YOUR DINNER.

OH! I CAN'T EAT THIS, MOM! MY HOMEWORK IS TO EAT A *CANDY BAR* FOR DINNER.

MINE TOO. BUT I THINK I HAVE ROOM FOR MEATBALLS AS WELL.

THEY DID *NOT* TELL YOU TO EAT A *CANDY BAR* FOR HOMEWORK!

OKAY, MOM.

ATTENTION, CLASS. I WILL NOW GRADE YOUR HOMEWORK. LINE UP FOR BIO-SCANNING.

BIO-SCAN OF NOAH KLAY HENRY REVEALS NO INDICATION OF CANDY BAR CONSUMPTION.

FAIL!

ZAP!

PASS...

PASS...

TWO CANDY BARS?

YEAH, DO I GET EXTRA CREDIT?

FAIL!

ZAP!

CAN'T YOU STOP THIS, COMPUTER JASON?

YEAH, I JUST NEED TO--

CONNECT TO ROBO SYSTEM

NO TALKING DURING BIO-SCANNING!

ZAP!

DATA LOST

YOU SHOULD BE INCAPACITATED!

I HAVE SUPER-POWERS.

DOES THIS MEAN I FAIL?

ERK!

COME BACK HERE AND SUBMIT TO ELECTRO-PUNISHMENT!

SORRY, I THINK I'LL PASS!

YOU ARE NOT SANCTIONED TO ASSIGN GRADES!

THE CENTRAL EASTERN UPSTATE SCHOOL DISTRICT TERMINATED THE ROBO-TEACHING PROGRAM TODAY AFTER A MALFUNCTION RESULTED IN THE ELECTROCUTION OF SEVERAL STUDENTS.

THE STUDENTS ARE BEING TREATED AT EASTERN UPSTATE HOSPITAL AND ARE EXPECTED TO MAKE FULL RECOVERIES.

FOR CHANNEL FOUR NEWS, I'M MITCH DYER.

NO, I'M AS SHOCKED AS *YOU* ARE! MY BOYS NEVER TELL ME *ANYTHING!*

CLASS, I'M SO HAPPY TO SEE YOU ALL AGAIN!

I GUESS THIS PROVES WHAT I'VE ALWAYS SAID -- ROBOTS WILL *NEVER* BE ABLE TO REPLACE HUMANS!

ALL OF YOUR FAILING GRADES WILL BE EXPUNGED FROM YOUR PERMANENT RECORD.

OH, THANK GOODNESS! NOW I STILL HAVE A CHANCE OF GETTING INTO A GOOD COLLEGE!

AND I'D LIKE TO GIVE A GOLD STAR TO THE YOUNG MAN WHO STOPPED THE ROBO-TEACHERS AND SAVED OUR JOBS.

COMPUTER JASON NEUTRALIZED THE ROBO-THREAT WITH HIS SUPERIOR INTELLECT AND HIS ADVANCED COMPUTER TECHNOLOGY.

IT IS A *PRIVILEGE* TO TEACH SUCH A BRIGHT STUDENT!

WOW. THANK YOU FOR THE STICKER.

AND *G-MAN.* IT SEEMS YOU PERPETRATED A CODE ALPHA RED.

I TRUST THERE IS NO NEED TO EXPLAIN WHAT THAT MEANS.

NOBODY HAS ANY IDEA WHAT THAT MEANS.

THE SCHOOL BOARD HAS DECIDED YOU ARE A DANGEROUS THREAT TO ALL, SO YOU ARE SUSPENDED UNTIL FURTHER REVIEW.

GET OUT OF HERE BEFORE YOU HOSPITALIZE US.

I CAN NEVER TELL IF I'M SMARTER OR DUMBER THAN EVERYONE ELSE.

THE END.

JUST JAMES in THE PLAYGROUND OF THE LIVING DEAD

BY

JOSH ELDER (STORY/SCRIPT)
JIM VARGAS (COLORS)

JASON ALLEN (STORY/PENCILS)
STEVE WALLACE (LETTERS)

... DO YOU THINK, JAMES? JAMES?

NARCISSUS

Comics will Rot your Braaaiinn

JAMES JEFFORDS!

HAHAH

HAHAH

HUH!

WHA!

NICE MOVES, SPAZ!

HAHHAA

HAHAH

DYLAN, WHY DO YOU HAVE TO BE SUCH A *JERK*?

I DON'T KNOW, KATIE. WHY DON'T YOU ASK *JAMES* WHY HE HAS TO BE SUCH A *WEIRDO*?

Allegory—A story with a deeper, symbolic meaning beyond its literal surface meaning

CLASS, DO I NEED TO SEND YOU ALL BACK TO THE 4TH GRADE? BECAUSE YOU'RE CERTAINLY *ACTING* LIKE YOU STILL BELONG THERE.

NO, MS. JOHNSON.

RIIIIING

YOUR *ALLEGORICAL* STORIES ARE DUE ON FRIDAY! DOUBLE-SPACED WITH 1-INCH MARGINS! AND DON'T THINK I WON'T GET OUT A RULER AND CHECK!

HOLD ON, JAMES. I NEED TO TAKE A LOOK AT WHAT YOU WERE DRAWING IN YOUR *TEXTBOOK* — WHERE YOU'RE NOT SUPPOSED TO MAKE MARKS OF *ANY* KIND — BEFORE I CAN LET YOU GO.

... YES, MA'AM. AND I WAS ... I WAS JUST GOOFING AROUND ...

YES, WHEN YOU WERE SUPPOSED TO BE PAYING ATTENTION IN CLASS. YOU'RE A VERY BRIGHT YOUNG MAN, JAMES, BUT NOT SO BRIGHT THAT YOU CAN DAYDREAM YOUR WAY TO A GOOD GRADE.

YES, MA'AM.

HMMMM. THAT'S A GOOD LIKENESS. THOUGH IT MAY SURPRISE YOU TO KNOW THAT I USED TO DRAW MY OWN COMICS WHEN I WAS YOUR AGE. STILL DO, IN FACT.

AND SINCE YOU LIKE DRAWING SO MUCH, I WANT YOU TO TELL YOUR 2-PAGE STORY WITH PICTURES AS WELL AS WORDS. THINK YOU CAN DO THAT?

Y-YES, MA'AM!

THE STORY CAN BE ABOUT ANYTHING YOU WANT, SO LONG AS IT'S REALLY ABOUT SOMETHING ELSE. SOMETHING THAT MATTERS TO YOU.

YEAH... I'VE GOT JUST THE THING...

INTRODUTION

BY MICHAEL LARICCIA

LEARN 5 DAMN!

SOC 106:
INTRODUCTION
TO SOCIAL
JUSTICE

OKAY, CLASS, LET'S GET STARTED.

H-H-HELLO EVERYONE.

M-M-Y NAME IS MS. RUSSELL, I MEAN DOCTOR RUSSELL.

OF COURSE, WE'LL USE A TEXTBOOK, BUT I'D LIKE TO CHALLENGE YOU TO 'ND ANOTHER LAYER.

MY MOTHER RAISED MY SISTER AND ME IN ABJECT POVERTY.

SHE TAUGHT US TO RECOGNIZE OPPORTUNITIES AND TO BE COGNIZANT OF LIFE'S HARSH REALITIES.

THOUGH I AM A PROFESSOR, I HAVE NOT FOUND *ALL* MY ANSWERS IN BOOKS.

INTRODUCTION TO SOCIAL JUSTICE

SO DO NOT GO SEARCHING FOR ALL OF THE ANSWERS IN THIS BOOK.

SOME OF YOU MAY BE STRUGGLING WITH THIS SUBJECT MATTER ON A VERY PERSONAL LEVEL.

IT WAS HARD FOR ME WHEN I STARTED TO BECOME AWARE OF SOCIAL INEQUITIES.

PEOPLE ASSUME THAT IF YOU ARE BLACK YOU ARE AUTOMATICALLY AWARE OF PREJUDICE.

CAN YOU TAKE OFF FOR A FEW HOURS? MY PARENTS DON'T KNOW THAT I HAVE A BLACK ROOMMATE.

I CAN'T BELIEVE THIS IS HAPPENING TO ME!

YOU KNOW JENNY ONLY HANGS OUT WITH YOU BECAUSE YOU'RE HER 'BLACK FRIEND,' RIGHT?

NOT TRUE...

BUT WHEN I WAS YOUR AGE, I STARTED SEEING THINGS DIFFERENTLY. AND IT MADE ME ANGRY AND UPSET.

FRUSTRATION AND BITTERNESS WERE WEIGHTS I CARRIED FOR MANY YEARS.

DR. RUSSELL, DID YOUR FRUSTRATION EVER MAKE YOU WANT TO, LIKE, GIVE UP?

I DID...

...MANY TIMES. BUT THANKFULLY I HAD A STRONG SUPPORT SYSTEM.

I'M NOT GOOD ENOUGH FOR GRAD SCHOOL!

THAT IS SO NOT TRUE. YOU GOT INTO ONE OF THE BEST SCHOOLS IN THE WORLD AND YOU GOT HERE WITH A THIRD OF THE RESOURCES!

MARIE, YOU HAVE A LOT TO OFFER TO THE FIELD.

DEAN BOWE

YOU SHOULD STICK WITH IT.

32

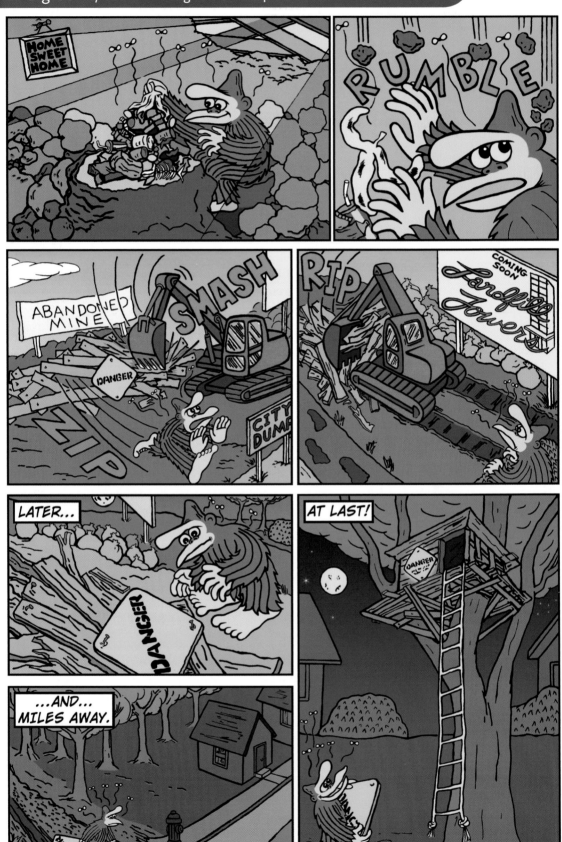

Our Backyard Field Guide by Stewart Morison and Todd Blakely

We weren't 100% sure how to do a field guide, so we went to the library yesterday and got this old one with weird pictures of guys in hunting gear smoking pipes and stuff like that. But it's also full of facts we can use today while we're observing and it even talks about how to track things – like a bear.

But before starting, I'm going to write down some things Mr. Rikagawa told us to remember (so we'll remember them!):

1) Choose a location. In this case, it's our backyard. We're lucky. We live pretty close to the woods and there's a stream and even a pond not too far from here.

2) Decide what kinds of facts will be included such as the scientific names for plants and animals. People will think you're smart and they sound cool if said fast!

3) Use drawings or photographs or both! We decided to use drawings for two reasons. The first reason is because we're both pretty good at drawing pictures.
The second is because Mom wouldn't let us borrow the camera.

4) Have LOTS of paper! A binder is good because you can put more and more paper in it as you add stuff. We chose graph paper because it looks more scientific.

We observe a bluejay –*Cyanocitta cristata* – and it really IS blue. They like to eat ALL kinds of bugs and seeds. It sits on a powerline. Why doesn't it fry?

A fly, one of MANY we saw around our tree house. This drawing is slightly bigger than life size.

A fat brown rat stood up and looked at us. *Rattus norvegicus* should not be confused with a mouse – which is much smaller... and connected to a PC.

I say it's melted pizza but Todd says it's vomit.

Common blue violets bloom all around the area.

A twig with little yellow flowery things on it. We think it is called SPICEBUSH but we didn't want to taste it to find out if it is really spicy or not.

THE EASTERN GREY SQUIRREL—also known scientifically as SCIURUS CAROLINENIS.
Squirrels are pretty common in this area. In fact, I've seen this squirrel before.

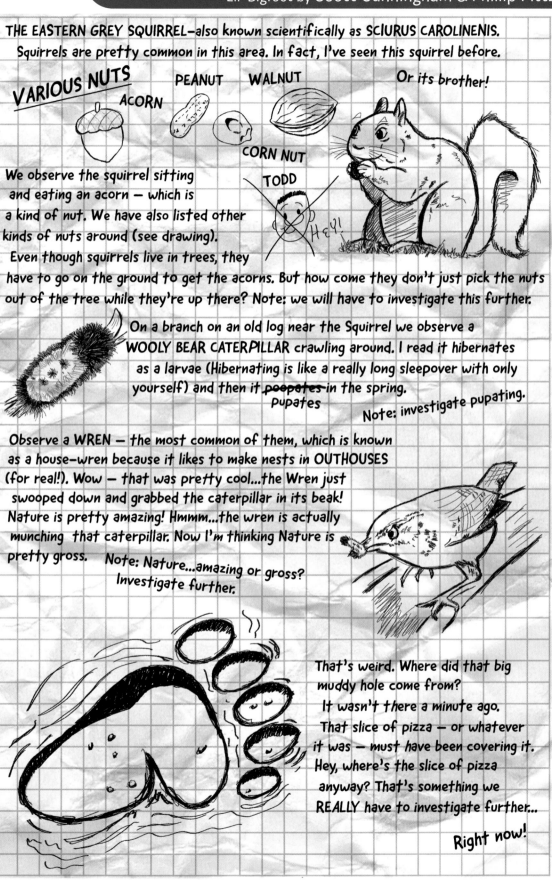

VARIOUS NUTS

ACORN   PEANUT   WALNUT   Or its brother!

CORN NUT

TODD

H E Y!

We observe the squirrel sitting
and eating an acorn — which is
a kind of nut. We have also listed other
kinds of nuts around (see drawing).
Even though squirrels live in trees, they
have to go on the ground to get the acorns. But how come they don't just pick the nuts
out of the tree while they're up there? Note: we will have to investigate this further.

On a branch on an old log near the Squirrel we observe a
WOOLY BEAR CATERPILLAR crawling around. I read it hibernates
as a larvae (Hibernating is like a really long sleepover with only
yourself) and then it ~~poopates~~ in the spring.
                    Pupates
                              Note: investigate pupating.

Observe a WREN — the most common of them, which is known
as a house-wren because it likes to make nests in OUTHOUSES
(for real!). Wow — that was pretty cool...the Wren just
swooped down and grabbed the caterpillar in its beak!
Nature is pretty amazing! Hmmm...the wren is actually
munching that caterpillar. Now I'm thinking Nature is
pretty gross.   Note: Nature...amazing or gross?
                 Investigate further.

That's weird. Where did that big
muddy hole come from?
It wasn't there a minute ago.
That slice of pizza — or whatever
it was — must have been covering it.
Hey, where's the slice of pizza
anyway? That's something we
REALLY have to investigate further...

Right now!

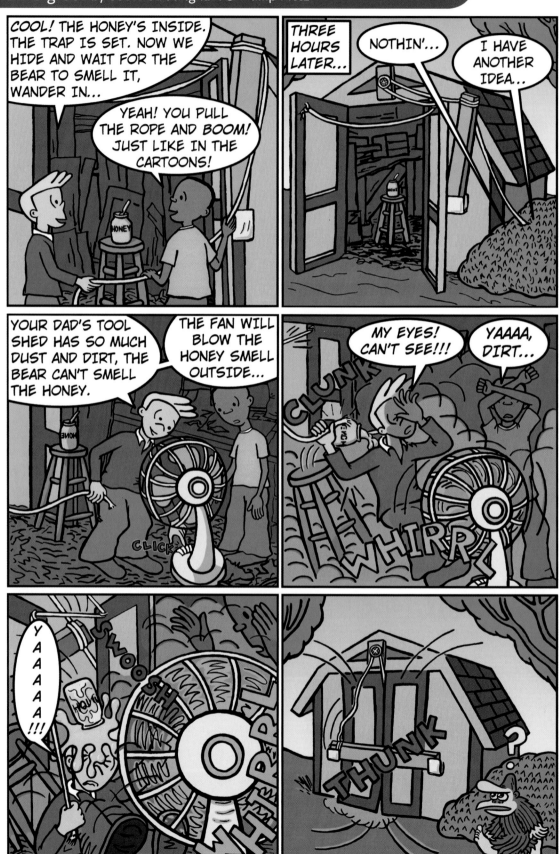

SETTING
WHERE: Cherry Creek, IN (Pop. 23,746)
WHEN: The Present Day

SO WHAT DO YOU THINK WE SHOULD PLAY TODAY, HERM? DUCK, DUCK, GENJUTSU? HOPSHURIKEN? DODGEBLADE?

I'LL HAVE TO ANSWER D) NONE OF THE ABOVE. I CAN'T QUIT READING NOW, NOT RIGHT IN THE MIDDLE OF THE CHAPTER ON MUSCLE AND BONE DENSITY!

L. Frank Baum

BIO
NAME: Timothy James McAllister
OCCUPATION: Student and Ninja Owner
FAVORITE ADJECTIVE: Ninjarific

BIO
NAME: Herman W. Poindexter
OCCUPATION: Timmy's best friend and all-around über-genius
WHY HE NEEDS GLASSES: Because he was blinded … with SCIENCE!

DUDE, THIS IS *RECESS!* ISN'T IT AGAINST THE *LAW* TO READ A BOOK DURING RECESS?

SOMEHOW I DOUBT THAT.

Physiology for Morons

WELL IT *SHOULD* BE! NOW STOP SITTING THERE AND GET UP SO WE CAN DO SOMETHING *AWESOME!*

WOOOOOOSH

INTELLECTUAL SELF-ACTUALIZATION IS THE EPITOME OF AWESOMENESS!

WOOOOOOOSH

YOU'RE JUST MAKING WORDS UP NOW!

THAT DOESN'T MAKE ANY SENSE AT ALL!

AM NOT! YOU'RE THE ONE WHO NEEDS TO BUY A *THESAURUS!*

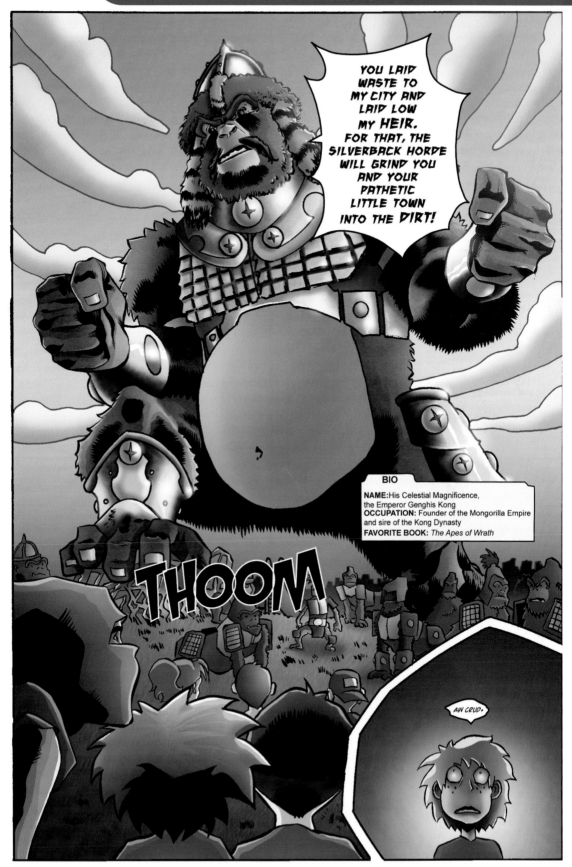

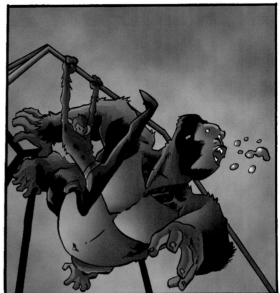

I SEE YOU HAVE DEFEATED MY MINIONS.

NOW LET US SEE HOW YOU FARE AGAINST THEIR MASTER!

OOH... *THAT'S* GONNA LEAVE A MARK.

INDUBITABLY.

FWACK!

SNAP

FOOT TO FACE

KRUNCH

TWHAP!

VICTORY!

THUMP! THUMP! THUMP!

NO WAY! JIRO CAN'T GET *PUNKED* BY SOME OVERGROWN MONKEY!

FIRST, GORILLAS AREN'T MONKEYS, THEY'RE APES. SECOND, THE *SQUARE-CUBE LAW* PROVES THAT IT'S IMPOSSIBLE FOR ANY MONKEY OR APE TO EVER GET *THAT* OVERGROWN.

THE SQUARE-CUBE LAW WAS FIRST FORMULATED BY *GALILEO* IN THE 17TH CENTURY, AND IT STATES THAT AS HEIGHT INCREASES...

...SURFACE AREA - WHICH DETERMINES *STRENGTH* - INCREASES BY A SQUARED FACTOR - WHILE VOLUME - WHICH DETERMINES *WEIGHT* - INCREASES BY A CUBED FACTOR.

125

25

5

HEIGHT   STRENGTH   WEIGHT

SO GENGHIS KONG IS 30 FT TALL, 5 TIMES TALLER THAN AN ORDINARY GORILLA.

WHAT... *SORCERY*... IS... *THIS?*

WHICH MEANS HIS STRENGTH IS 5^2 OR *25* TIMES GREATER THAN THAT OF AN ORDINARY GORILLA, BUT HIS WEIGHT IS 5^3 OR *125* TIMES GREATER THAN THAT OF AN ORDINARY GORILLA.

FEEL... *SO... HEAVY...*

WHY AT THAT HEIGHT, HE WOULDN'T EVEN HAVE THE STRENGTH TO *STAND UPRIGHT*, MUCH LESS FIGHT ANYONE.

SCIENCE SAYS THAT IT'S *IMPOSSIBLE*, AND YOU CAN'T ARGUE WITH *SCIENCE*.

THUD

WAY TO GO, GUYS! TOTAL *APE*-POCALYPSE!

THIS VICTORY DOES NOT BELONG TO US.

IT WAS *BRAINS* THAT FELLED THE BEAST.

AW, IT'S NO BIG DEAL. GALILEO WAS THE ONE WHO DID ALL THE HARD WORK ANYWAY...

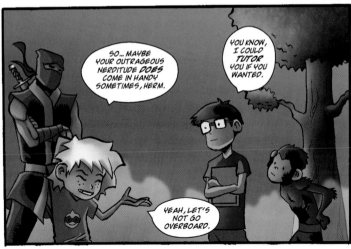

SO... MAYBE YOUR OUTRAGEOUS NERDITUDE *DOES* COME IN HANDY SOMETIMES, HERM.

YOU KNOW, I COULD *TUTOR* YOU IF YOU WANTED.

YEAH, LET'S NOT GO OVERBOARD.

AND HEY, WE'VE STILL GOT 10 MINUTES OF RECESS LEFT! WHO'S UP FOR SOME *DODGEBLADE?!*

SO MUCH MORE
TORY WOOLLCOTT

EVERYONE, YOU'RE GOING TO BE READING FROM CHAPTER FOUR.

WHEN YOU CAN'T READ, YOU DON'T REALLY UNDERSTAND WHAT YOU'RE MISSING.

YOU KNOW THERE'S SOMETHING THERE, SOMETHING EVERYONE ELSE CAN SEE, BUT YOU JUST CAN'T. I THINK IT'S A LOT LIKE BEING COLORBLIND AND HAVING EVERYONE TELL YOU THAT YOU WOULD REALLY LIKE RED IF YOU WOULD JUST TRY HARD ENOUGH TO SEE IT.

VICTORIA, WOULD YOU STAY BEHIND? I'D LIKE TO TALK TO YOU.

I'VE NOTICED THAT YOU'RE HAVING TROUBLE READING.

I'M FINE.

THEN COULD YOU READ THIS PARAGRAPH FOR ME?

THE BOY IS... NA-NAME-ED... NAMED... THE BOY IS NAMED FOR HIS...

I THINK THAT'S ENOUGH. VICTORIA, YOU JUST AREN'T READING AT YOUR GRADE LEVEL. I KNOW THAT YOU'RE A BRIGHT GIRL AND THAT YOU TRY HARD, BUT YOU JUST KEEP FALLING BEHIND.

I WANT TO HELP YOU, BUT YOU'RE GOING TO HAVE TO TELL ME HOW.

...

WELL...

I DON'T KNOW... IT'S JUST...

...THE WORDS MOVE AROUND ON THE PAGE...

...LIKE UGLY LITTLE ANTS. I CAN'T KEEP THEM STRAIGHT.

THAT'S WHY I ALWAYS HAVE TO READ WITH SOMEONE ELSE. I GUESS I'M JUST DUMB.

I DON'T SEE WHAT THE BIG DEAL IS... READING IS BORING AND STUPID.

NO IT ISN'T STUPID...

...AND NEITHER ARE YOU.

READING DOESN'T COME EASY FOR YOU LIKE IT DOES FOR SOME PEOPLE, AND THAT MAKES YOU FEEL FRUSTRATED. IT MAKES YOU WANT TO GIVE UP, BUT THAT MEANS YOU'D BE GIVING UP ON A LOT OF GREAT STORIES AND A LOT OF GREAT IDEAS THAT CAN ONLY BE FOUND IN BOOKS.

I THINK YOU'RE GETTING LOST BECAUSE THERE ARE TOO MANY WORDS ON THE PAGE. IT MAKES YOU LOSE TRACK OF THE STORY.

BECAUSE YOU WERE BRAVE ENOUGH TO TELL US ABOUT YOUR PROBLEM, WE CAN WORK TOGETHER TO FIND WAYS TO FIX IT.

THE FIRST STEP IS TO GET YOU TO STOP HATING BOOKS AND READING IN GENERAL.

AND I THINK I KNOW HOW.

WOW.

Comics for Kids!

EXCUSE ME, I'M LOOKING FOR SOME CHILD-APPROPRIATE BOOKS.

MY DAUGHTER HAS BEEN HAVING TROUBLE READING, AND I THOUGHT COMICS MIGHT HELP.

IT LOOKS LIKE YOUR DAUGHTER AGREES!

OH COOL!

I REALLY WANT HER TO HAVE A LOVE OF BOOKS. SHE LOVES STORIES, AND I'M WORRIED THAT HER READING DIFFICULTIES WILL KEEP HER FROM EXPERIENCING ALL THE WONDERFUL STORIES SHE COULD FIND INSIDE OF BOOKS.

...BECAUSE THEY USE MORE THAN JUST WORDS TO TELL A STORY.

COMICS AND GRAPHIC NOVELS APPEAL TO RELUCTANT READERS AND KIDS WITH LEARNING DISABILITIES...

sky dog comics
skydogcomics.com   ☐ SHOT FOR COLOR TITLE:_____   PAGE_____
☐ SHOT FOR CODE   PENCILER:_____   INKER:_____   INTERIORS

HOW YA GONNA DRAW:  BY RICH FABER

STEP 1: BEGIN WITH A SIMPLE FRAMEWORK. A STICK FIGURE WILL DO THE TRICK!

ADD CIRCLES FOR ROBOY'S HEAD AND HANDS, AND OVALS FOR HIS BODY AND FEET.

REMEMBER TO DRAW GUIDELINES FOR THE FEATURES ON ROBOY'S FACE!

STEP 2: USE GUIDELINES TO ADD CIRCLES FOR HIS EYES. 4 TRIANGLES ON TOP OF HIS HEAD MAKE UP ROBOY'S SPIKEY HAIR!

ROBOY'S FACE IS HEART SHAPED. KEEP THAT IN MIND WHEN DRAWING HIS EAR, CHEEK AND CHIN.

CONNECT HIS FEET AND HANDS TO HIS BODY TO CREATE ARMS AND LEGS. HEY, LOOK! IT'S STARTING TO LOOK LIKE ROBOY!

STEP 3: WHEW! HALFWAY THERE! TIME TO ADD HIS EYEBALLS, EYEBROWS AND HAIRLINE.

OH YEAH... DON'T FORGET HIS NOSE AND MOUTH!

DRAW SOME FINGERS AND GLOVES ON THOSE HANDS AND THE TOPS OF ROBOY'S BOOTS. ADD THE SHOULDER PADS, AND WE'RE READY FOR...

STEP 4: OK, IT'S TIME TO ERASE YOUR GUIDELINES.

NOW, DRAW HIGHLIGHTS IN HIS EYES, THE INSIDE OF HIS EAR, AND OTHER DETAILS.

REMEMBER ROBOY'S LIGHTNING BOLTS, AND OF COURSE, HIS TAIL!

STEP 5: WE'RE ALMOST THERE! OOPS, ALMOST FORGOT HIS JETPACK!

OK, NOW DARKEN YOUR DRAWING. SHADE IN ROBOY'S EYEBROWS AND HIS EYEBALLS. ADD SHADOWS AS NEEDED.

ADD SOME HIGHLIGHTS TO HIS BODY, LEG, AND THE BOOTS, AND WE'RE JUST ABOUT READY FOR...

STEP 6: THIS IS IT! IF YOU WANT, YOU CAN GET OUT YOUR MARKERS OR PENS, AND TRY TO INK ROBOY. ADD YOUR SIGNATURE, AND YOU'RE DONE! CONGRATULATIONS! YOU'VE JUST DRAWN YOUR FIRST ROBOY RED!

ROBOY RED IS © AND ™2010 RICH FABER AND JOHN GALLAGHER

INSTRUCTIONS FOR DOUBLE PAGE SPREAD: CUT AS SHOWN, ABUT PAGE EDGES, TAPE ON BACK. DO NOT OVERLAP.
ALL BLEED ART MUST EXTEND TO SOLID LINE.
← CUT RIGHT-HAND PAGE AT THIS LINE   CUT LEFT-HAND PAGE AT THIS LINE →

A CONVERSATION
I HAD WHILE TEACHING A COMICS CLASS

TODAY, WE'RE GOING TO DESIGN COVERS FOR THE COMICS YOU GUYS MADE.

BE SURE THEY HAVE A TITLE, YOUR NAME, AND AN IMAGE OF SOME SORT.

BY RAINA TELGEMEIER

CAN I PUT A PRICE ON MINE?

GO FOR IT.

Jose's comic is AWESOME
by Jose
$1.99 U.S.
$2.99 Canada

HOW COME THINGS COST MORE IN CANADA?

IT'S NOT THAT THEY **COST** MORE...

IT'S THAT THE VALUE OF THE CANADIAN DOLLAR IS LESS THAN THAT OF THE AMERICAN DOLLAR.

SOMEWHERE OFF THE COAST OF TAZMANIA.

MAYDAY! MAYDAY! DIVER IN DISTRESS! OVER!

CAPT'N ELI HERE! I READ YOU. I'M ZEROING IN ON YOUR POSITION NOW!

THE MYSTERIES AND DANGERS OF THE SEA ARE AS ENDLESS AS THE OCEAN ITSELF. AS CAPT'N ELI AND CREW DISCOVER WHEN THEY MEET...

THE GOBLIN OF THE DEEP! STORY AND ART-JAY PISCOPO

...SOME KIND OF SEA MONSTER!... DIVER ISN'T RESPONDING!...

SEA MONSTER?

(SSHH!) HANG ON! WE'RE ON OUR WAY!

SOON.

THESE FOLKS ARE AMATEUR OCEANOGRAPHERS.

LOOKS LIKE THEY GOT IN WAY OVER THEIR HEADS.

HMM, THE LINE IS CUT, BUT THE SHARK PROOF CAGE IS INTACT.

NO DIVER.

HEY! THERMAL VENTS! JUST LIKE "OLD FAITHFUL" BUT UNDERWATER!

WHOA!

NOW THAT'S A BIG ONE!

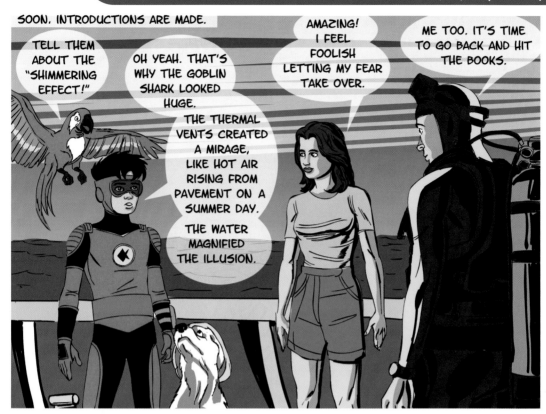

SOON, INTRODUCTIONS ARE MADE.

TELL THEM ABOUT THE "SHIMMERING EFFECT!"

OH YEAH. THAT'S WHY THE GOBLIN SHARK LOOKED HUGE.

THE THERMAL VENTS CREATED A MIRAGE, LIKE HOT AIR RISING FROM PAVEMENT ON A SUMMER DAY.

THE WATER MAGNIFIED THE ILLUSION.

AMAZING! I FEEL FOOLISH LETTING MY FEAR TAKE OVER.

ME TOO. IT'S TIME TO GO BACK AND HIT THE BOOKS.

LUCKY THIS ONE DIDN'T BECOME EXTINCT!

AYE, ROGER! THIS MUST BE YOUR UNDERWATER CAMERA I FOUND.

THE GOBLIN SHARK IS RARE, ESPECIALLY AT THE DEPTH YOU FOUND HIM.

HE DOES HAVE A STARTLING APPEARANCE. SO , WITH THE ILLUSION OF BEING A GIANT, I CAN SEE WHY YOU PANICKED.

GOBLIN SHARKS ARE "LIVING FOSSILS."

THAT MEANS THEY RESEMBLE AN EXTINCT SPECIES, WITH NO LIVING RELATIVE SPECIES.

PLEASE, NEXT TIME YOU "SHOOT" AT A GOBLIN SHARK, USE THIS.

THE END!

Loopy and the Nose of Misfortune!

Written by Camilla Zhang   Pencils by Tim Smith 3
Inks & Colors by Irene Y. Lee   Letters by Charlie Beckerman
Edited by Brandon Montclare

MIZ HENDRICKS! LOOPY'S ACTIN' ALL WEIRD AGAIN!

MY NAME IS *GUADALUPE STEIN.*

WHEN I WAS FIVE I HAD A MISSION. I WANTED TO BE MORE LIKEABLE... LESS *DIFFERENT.*

OBVIOUSLY, WITH A NAME LIKE "LOOPY", THE TASK REQUIRED A MIRACLE.

MY MOM CALLED ME "LUPITA ZEN." SOUNDS COOLER, DOESN'T IT? LIKE THE NAME OF A ROCK STAR.

IF ONLY IT STUCK DURING SCHOOL HOURS.

FOR THE LONGEST TIME, I NEVER REALLY UNDERSTOOD WHY MOM AND I DIDN'T LOOK MORE ALIKE...

...EVEN THOUGH I KNEW I WAS *ADOPTED.*

I ABSOLUTELY ADORED AND IDOLIZED MY MOTHER.

SO DID EVERYONE ELSE.

AS FAR AS I COULD TELL, THE ONLY STARK DIFFER-ENCES BETWEEN US WERE:

1. HOW PEOPLE *TREATED* US AND...

2. OUR *NOSES.*

IT DIDN'T HELP THAT NO ONE ELSE IN MY CLASS HAD A NOSE LIKE MINE.

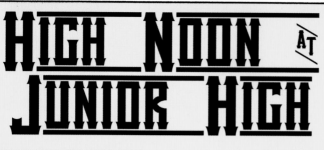

—BECAUSE I'VE DONE MY *HOMEWORK.*

— LAST NIGHT IT WAS JUST HALF AN HOUR OF VIDEO GAMES—

—AND HALF AN HOUR ON MYFACE.

THEN I HIT THE BOOKS.

HARD.

ALRIGHT CLASS, PLEASE TURN YOUR BOOKS TO CHAPTER 7.

NOW, THE UNITED STATES DECLARED WAR ON SPAIN APRIL 25TH, 1898.

CAN ANYONE TELL ME WHAT PROMINENT FIGURE HAD A HAND IN THAT DECISION?

(SIGH) YES, FR—

*

OH!

YES, WILL?

WELL I THINK IT'S PRETTY CLEAR WHO GETS *TODAY'S* GOLD STAR!

CONGRATULATIONS ON A JOB WELL DONE, WILL.

KANE, KANE, KANE!!

GO WILL!!

AWESOME!

LET'S SEE YOU DO THAT *TOMORROW*, HOT SHOT.

I'LL BE READY.

THE FURTHER ADVENTURES OF
FRANKIE PICKLE
"THE BEAST THAT SNORED" By Eric Wight

FRANKIE, AREN'T YOU WORRIED THAT READING **SCARY COMICS** BEFORE BED WILL GIVE YOU NIGHTMARES?

AW, MOM! I'M OLD ENOUGH TO KNOW THAT **MONSTERS** AREN'T REAL.

OF COURSE YOU ARE, SWEETIE.

08:57

I COULD READ THIS ALL NIGHT!

09:13

...ZZZ...

FUN FACT: The term *onomatopoeia* comes from the Greek word onomatopoiia, which literally means 'word-making.' How many *onomatopoeias* can you find in Frankie's adventure?

PROMOTING INTERGALACTIC LEARNING AND LEADERSHIP THROUGH STUDENT EXCHANGE PROGRAMS, ALBERT THE ALIEN ATTENDS SCHOOL ON EARTH TO LEARN AS HUMANS DO....

YESTERDAY WE TALKED ABOUT THE FIERCEST DINOSAUR OF THE CRETACEOUS PERIOD, THE TYRANNO-SAURUS REX.

TODAY WE'LL BE TALKING ABOUT THE AVIARY CREATURES OF THAT ERA.

YOU'LL RECALL FROM LAST NIGHT'S READING THAT PTEROSAURS MORE CLOSELY RESEMBLE MODERN DAY BIRDS THAN REPTILES

THEIR BONES WERE HOLLOW AND FILLED WITH AIR, AND THEY HAD WINGS FORMED BY A MEMBRANE OF SKIN AND OTHER TISSUES.

SOME SPECIES, LIKE THE QUETZALCOATLUS, HAD A WINGSPAN OF 30-40 FEET AND WERE AMONG THE LARGEST FLYING ANIMALS TO EVER LIVE.

Albert the Alien is New in School
Story: Trevor Mueller
Art: Gabo
Colors: Kevin Harrell

-OH, ALBERT DO YOU HAVE A QUESTION?

YES, TEACHER MR. SCHAFER. INSTEAD OF JUST READING ABOUT DINOSAURS, WHY DO WE NOT JUST GO TO THIS CRETACEOUS PERIOD AND SEE THEM?

DON'T BE STUPID, ALIEN! NO ON CAN GO BACK IN TIME.

SHUT UP, WALLY.

UNFORTUNATELY OUR PLANET DOESN'T HAVE THE TECHNOLOGY TO DO THAT SORT OF THING, ALBERT –

FORTUNATELY MY PLANET DOES, AND I NEVER LEAVE HOME WITHOUT MY DUROLEX 450 TIME SHIFTER!

FFZZZZ

FWOOOSH!

SECURE ANY LOOSE ITEMS AND PREPARE YOURSELVES FOR-

VERY TRUE. NOW IN CLASS TODAY WE LEARNED THAT PTEROSAURS WERE THE ANCESTORS OF MODERN DAY BIRDS.

RIGHT! AND OUR HOMEWORK SAID THEY SPENT THEIR DAY SEARCHING FOR FOOD FOR THEIR BABIES!

MAYBE IF YOU WEREN'T SUCH A BABY IT WOULD'VE TAKEN YOU....

AN EXCELLENT OBSERVATION, CLASSMATE WALLY! MR. SCHAFER WEIGHS SIGNIFICANTLY MORE THAN I DO, SO HE COULD NOT HAVE BEEN TAKEN FAR.

IF WE ARE ABLE TO EXTRAPOLATE THE PTEROSAUR'S HUNTING RADIUS, THEN WE CAN CALCULATE THE APPROXIMATE LOCATION OF THE NEST.

BLAH BLAH BLAH. YOU CAN EX- TRAPOLATE MY FOOT IN YOUR BUTT.

I WOULD NOT REC- OMMEND IT. I HAVE AN IDEA—

I'LL FIND THE TEACH MYSELF, AND THEN I'M GOIN' HOME

THE TEACHER WAS TAKEN IN THE OTHER DIRECTION, YOU JERK!

WHATEVER. LATER, LOSERS.

USE THIS TO CONTACT ME IF YOU NEED TO.

WHAT ARE YOU GOING TO DO?

CHUNK! KSSHH! SHUCK!

I'M GOING TO SAVE OUR TEACHER.

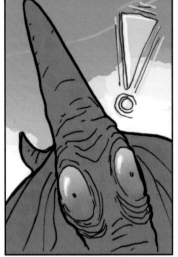

CHRONAL DISPLACEMENT REVERSED!!

-ZZZZZZZZZMM

-ZZZZZZZZZMM

AS EDUCATIONAL AS THAT WAS, ALBERT, I THINK YOU SHOULD KEEP YOUR TIME SHIFTER AT HOME FROM NOW ON.

I DID NOT REALIZE THAT OUR JOURNEY WOULD BE MORE DANGEROUS THAN NAPO FISHING DURING SPAWNING SEASON.

NEXT TIME, I WILL STICK TO LEARNING THE HUMAN WAY.

DON'T LOOK SO DOWN, ALBERT. IT WAS A LITTLE CRAZY, BUT THAT WAS STILL THE BEST FIELD TRIP EVER.

REALLY?

DEFINITELY. AND HEY, AT LEAST WE ALL MADE IT BACK IN ONE PIECE, RIGHT?

MEANWHILE, BACK IN THE CRETACEOUS PERIOD....

-RRAAARRRR!!

THIS IS ALL YOUR FAULT, ALIEN!

THE END

THE SIGNS ARE ALL IN PLACE.

A RECESS-DESTROYING DOWNPOUR.

THE ORDER OF THE SILENT Pencil

MS. GURTLE, THE MOST VILLIANOUS OF LUNCH AIDES.

LET THE SECRET ORDER CONVENE ONCE AGAIN.

WRITTEN, INKED AND COLORED by KEVIN PYLE   PENCILED by KEVIN SACCO   DRAWINGS by CALVIN PYLE

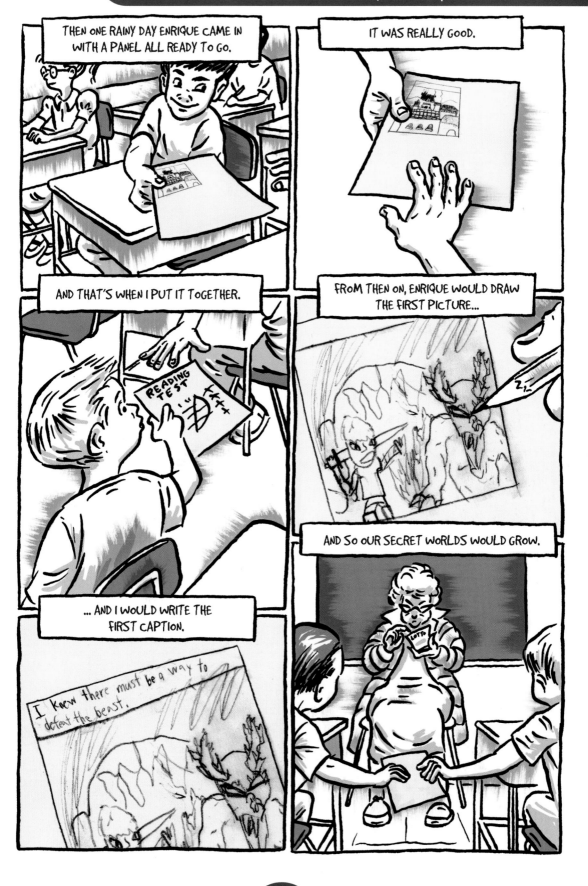

THE LEGEND OF BiLLY...
KiD BARBARiAN WANNABE!!

STORY & ART
DAVID REDDICK
COLORS BY DON KUEHN

BILLY, COME ON, IT'S TIME TO GO TO THE **LIBRARY** TO CHECK OUT A **BOOK** FOR **CLASS!**

BOOKS? HA! WHAT DOES A **BARBARIAN** NEED WITH **BOOKS,** FRANKY?!

THERE'S NO TIME FOR **READING** WHEN YOU'RE **HACKING AND SLASHING** YOUR WAY TO **VICTOROUS ADVENTURE!!**

BILLY, FOR THE **MILLIONTH** TIME, YOU'RE **NOT** A BARBARIAN. YOU'RE JUST A **KID** WHO'S **PARENTS** WORK AS CASTLE **TAX ACCOUNTANTS.**

WELL, **I'M** GONNA BE **DIFFERENT!** **I'M** GONNA BE A **GREAT BARBARIAN** WHO **TRAVELS** THE **FOUR KINGDOMS** IN SEARCH OF **AWESOMENESS...**

...AND **CANDY!**

TRAVEL THE FOUR KINGDOMS?! **HA!!** WHERE WILL YOU **GO?** YOU'VE NEVER EVEN BEEN **OUTSIDE** YOUR **OWN VILLAGE!**

YOU **KNOW**, FRANKY, **MOST** DRAGONS ARE JUST **DUMB**, FIRE-BREATHING **LIZARDS** WITH **BAD BREATH**... WHY CAN'T **YOU** BE MORE LIKE **THEM**?

BECAUSE I **READ**.

SO, BILLY, WHERE'S THE **FIRST** PLACE YOU'LL GO IN SEARCH OF ALL THIS **ADVENTURE**?

I'LL GO... I MEAN... THAT IS... **THAT** WAY... YES, THAT WAY SEEMS LIKE THE MOST **ADVENTUROUS** CHOICE!

YOU HAVE **NO** **IDEA**, DO YOU?

NOPE.

IF ONLY I HAD SOME **MAGIC SPELL** OR SOME **ENCHANTED COMPASS** TO GUIDE ME ON MY WAY TO ADVENTURE!

THERE ARE **WHISPERS**, BILLY, YES, WHISPERS OF JUST SUCH AN **OBJECT**... SOMETHING WITH GREAT **POWER** THAT CAN **GUIDE** YOU TO YOUR **DREAM**...

WHERE CAN I FIND SUCH AN **OBJECT**?! **SHOW ME, FRANKY!!**

LIBRARY

HOW TO TRAIN YOUR BARBARIAN

GEOGRAPHY FOR WANNABE BARBARIANS

www.LegendofBill.com

UNSHELVED SECRET ORIGINS
by Gene Ambaum & Bill Barnes

Dewey

ONE OF MY FIRST MEMORIES IS OF COMICS.

HOW TO CHANGE A BABY

1. 2. 3. 4.

HOLD STILL OR I'M GETTING THE STAPLE GUN!

I QUICKLY INFERRED ALL THE RULES OF GRAMMAR.

IT'S BIRD PLANE SUPER

I LEARNED A LOT OF VOCABULARY

%¿#@!

I FOUND THINGS TO ASPIRE TO.

SOMEDAY I'M GOING TO OWN A CAT AND BE ABLE TO READ IT'S MIND!

GARFELD GETS REPETITIV

Unshelved: Secret Origins by Gene Ambaum & Bill Barnes

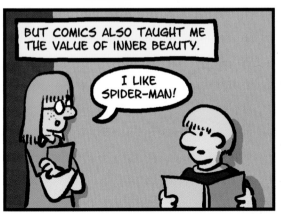

I THOUGHT ABOUT BECOMING A *SCIENTIST*.

TAKING OVER THE WORLD SOUNDS LIKE A LOT OF *WORK*

I CONSIDERED A CAREER AS AN *ASTRONAUT*.

MOW THE LAWN *NOW* OR I'LL KNOCK YOU INTO *SPACE*!

BUT COMICS TAUGHT ME IT'S IMPORTANT TO GO WHERE I'M *NEEDED*.

LIBRARY

YOU? A LIBRARIAN? HA!

COMICS? HERE? OVER MY DEAD BODY!

SMALLVILLE ADVERTISER

LOCAL LIBRARIAN FINALLY CHECKS OUT

BODY DEAD

AND HERE I AM!

WHO WANTS SOME COMICS?

I'LL SHOW HIM! I'M GOING TO READ A BOOK THAT'S FULL OF *WORDS*!

JUST WORDS.

THE END... OR IS IT?

BONUS! THE SECRET ORIGIN OF COMICS!

YOU GOT PICTURES IN MY WORDS!

YOU GOT WORDS IN MY PICTURES!

GA

BB

ONCE UPON A TIME, A BOY FELL ASLEEP AND DREAMT OF A LAND OF ELVES, FAIRIES AND DRAGONS...

THE DREAMLAND CHRONICLES

WRITTEN AND ILLUSTRATED BY SCOTT CHRISTIAN SAVA

BLUE DREAM

WWW.THEDREAMLANDCHRONICLES.COM

The Dreamland Chronicles

WWW.THEDREAMLANDCHRONICLES.COM

HEY, NASTAJIA. WHAT'CHA *READING?*

JANE AUSTEN'S *PRIDE AND PREJUDICE.*

OH! I *ADORE* THAT BOOK!

ISN'T IT *AMAZING,* KIWI?

WHAT'S IT *ABOUT?* ARE THERE *ZOMBIES* IN IT?

ZOMBIES? NO...IT'S ABOUT...

OH! OH! DOES...DOES IT HAVE *SEA MONSTERS?*

HEAVENS NO! THERE'S ABSOLUTELY *NO* ZOMBIES AND *NO* SEA MONSTERS!

106

IT'S A **BRILLIANT** WORK OF LITERATURE SET IN PRE-VICTORIAN ENGLAND ABOUT AN **INDEPENDENT** WOMAN...

...OVERCOMING HER **SOCIAL STATUS** WHILE DISCOVERING A DEEP AND **PASSIONATE** LOVE THAT BREAKS THE SHACKLES OF CLASS AND SOCIETAL **HIERARCHY.**

HEY PADDINGTON. I'VE GOT A **SWORD**... WANT TO GO **STAB** THINGS?

OK.

GIRLS ARE **WEIRD,** PADDINGTON.

BOYS ARE **STUPID,** KIWI.

Dr. Stevelove
Or how I learned to stop worrying and talk to girls
A Matriculated Flashback by Phil Chan & Joe Dunn

I'll call you tonight, ok?

Sure! See ya!

What up, Dan?

How do you do that, Steve?

Do what?

Talk to girls like that.

Well, I open my mouth and sound comes out.

You know what I mean. How can you so casually just talk to girls?

Sometimes I try to talk to girls and I feel like I've forgotten the English language.

Like I would probably be better off if I *literally* put my foot in my mouth, y'know?

But you just walk up to them and talk like it's a normal thing.

It *is* a normal thing.

In Stevetown, maybe, but in Danville there's a little thing called "making a fool of yourself". What's your secret?

Listen close, mi compadre, I'm going to take you back to a simpler time.

I'm going to tell you a story that will, no joke, change your life.

After years of being too timid to even approach her, that bit of hearsay gave me the courage to finally go and talk to her.

But, it was a big party.

I looked and I looked, but she was nowhere to be found.

I spent the rest of the night looking for her...

...but I never found her.

You know how you look back on your life and you can pick out a few moments that defined you?

That night at the graduation party was one of those.

5TH PERIOD MRS. JONES' HONORS CIVICS

END OF DAY — AMY'S LOCKER

WHERE IS SHE?

AMBER! HEY, HAVE YOU SEEN --

AMY TOLD ME TO TELL YOU THAT SHE DOESN'T WANT TO GO OUT WITH YOU ANYMORE.

B-BUT SHE'S THE ONE WHO ASKED ME...

YEAH...SHE ONLY SAID THAT BECAUSE SHE FELT SORRY FOR YOU.

BUT...

IT'S HER LOSS REALLY; LOTS OF GIRLS WANT TO, YOU KNOW, GO OUT WITH YOU.

WAIT, WHAT?

YEAH. I MEAN...

I WOULD GO OUT WITH YOU.

YOU WOULD?

YES.

ONE DAY WITH AMY

WORDS: STEVE WALLACE
ART: DANIEL GUTOWSKI

DRENCHED, LOADED AND *DANGEROUS!*

WHAT IF MR. KILSOME IS A MONSTER

MRS. DOUGHTY... THAT *JERK* HIT ME WITH A SPITBALL...

AGAIN!!!

MR. MAGINE, I'M *THROUGH* GIVING YOU WARNINGS

YOU *MARCH* YOURSELF RIGHT DOWN TO *MR. KILSOME'S* OFFICE, NOW.

???WWHHIIZZTT

MR. KILSOME... YOUR GONNA *GET IT* NOW

THAT'S ENOUGH JENNIFER.

WILLY YOU GET MOVING... *NOW MARCH!!!*

I WONDER WHY JENNIFER THOUGHT ME SEEING MR. KILSOME WOULD BE SO BAD. WHAT IF...

THE ONE THING WE SHOULD NOTE ABOUT WILLY IS THAT LATE AT NIGHT ON THE WEEKEND, HE ENJOYED SNEAKING DOWNSTAIRS WHEN HIS PARENTS WERE ASLEEP AND TURNING ON THE TELEVISION TO WATCH THE LATE-LATE-MONSTER-MASH-UP. THAT BEING THE CASE, IT'S NO SURPRISE THAT WILLY CAME TO THE CONCLUSION THAT MR. KILLSOME IS A MONSTER!!!

THAT'S BRUNNO SACKS, THE *MEANEST* BULLY IN THE SIXTH GRADE, LEAVING MR. KILSOME'S OFFICE...

AND HE'S *CRYING!!!*

UH OH!

MR. KILSOME MUST BE REALLY, *REALLY* SCARY.

UM... MRS. DOUGHTER TOLD ME TO COME DOWN HERE.

COME IN AND SIT *DOWN.*

THAT DAY WILLY FOUND OUT THAT MR. KILSOME WAS THE *WORST* KIND OF MONSTER OF ALL.

THE KIND THAT *CALLED* UP YOUR PARENTS AND TOLD THEM WHEN YOU HAD BEEN *BAD.*

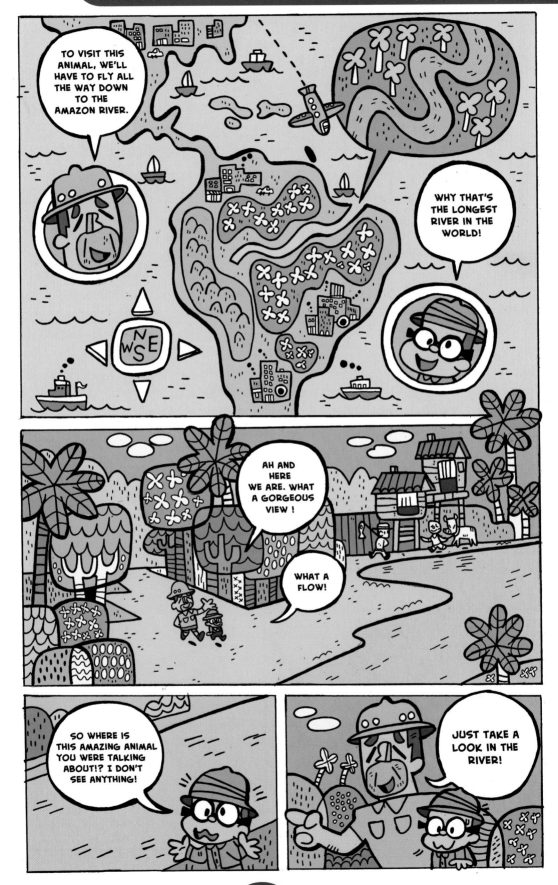

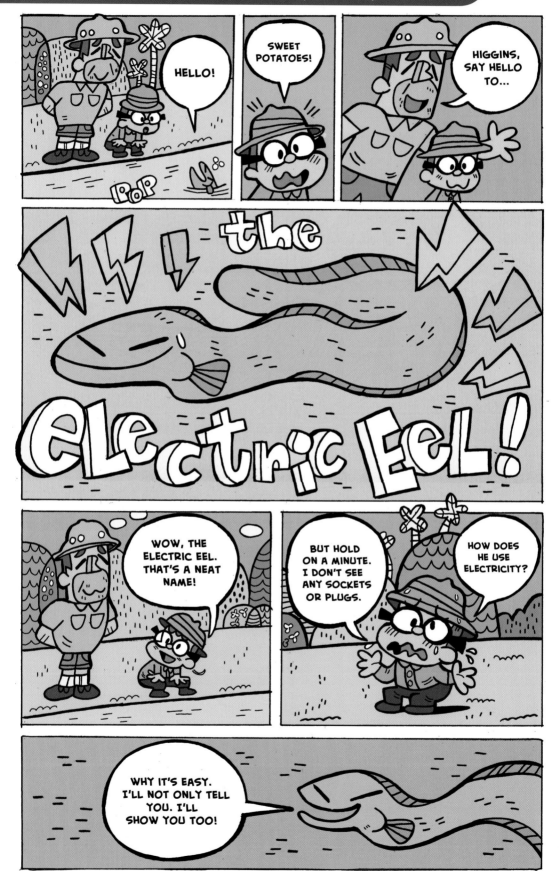

YOU SEE I HAVE SPECIAL ORGANS IN MY BODY THAT GIVE ME THE ABILITY TO CREATE AN ELECTRIC CURRENT!

I CAN EVEN STORE THIS ELECTRICITY INSIDE ME LIKE A BATTERY.

OUCH!

WHEN I GET CLOSE TO MY PREY ALL I HAVE TO DO IS GIVE THEM A GOOD ZAP.

I CAN DELIVER UP TO

500 VOLTS

OF ELECTRICITY!

WHOA!

500 VOLTS?! THAT'S FIVE TIMES STRONGER THEN THE ELECTRICITY IN THE WALL SOCKETS AT HOME!

REMIND ME NOT TO GO SWIMMING WITH THIS GUY!

HEY, HERE COME SOME TASTY FISH RIGHT NOW!

BLUB

BLUB

BLUB

LOOK OUT HIGGINS, THIS EEL IS READY TO COOK HIS LUNCH!

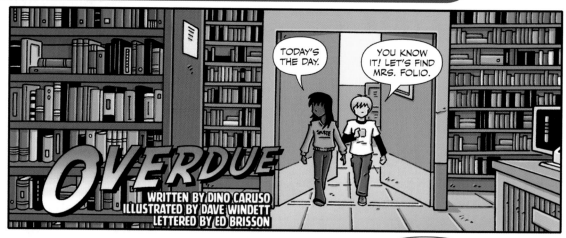

OVERDUE

WRITTEN BY DINO CARUSO
ILLUSTRATED BY DAVE WINDETT
LETTERED BY ED BRISSON

TODAY'S THE DAY.

YOU KNOW IT! LET'S FIND MRS. FOLIO.

MRS. FOLIO... DID THE NEW GRAPHIC NOVELS COME IN YET?

THE MANGA? THE SUPERHEROES? THE FUNNY ONE WITH THE TALKING MOUSE?

ERRR...WELL, THERE'S BEEN A DELAY. A PROBLEM WITH THE DELIVERY TRUCK I THINK. YES! THAT'S IT. THE TRUCK WAS HELD UP IN A...A... A SNOWSTORM.

SNOWSTORM?

IN THE MIDDLE OF MAY?

RIGHT THEN. RUN ALONG CHILDREN. BACK TO CLASS WITH YOU.

BUT... BUT...

MRS. FOLIO, THE WHOLE SCHOOL HAS BEEN WAITING FOR THE GRAPHIC NOVELS TO ARRIVE!

YES, YES, I'LL BE SURE TO MAKE AN ANNOUNCEMENT WHEN THE BOOKS ARE ON THE SHELF.

GOODBYE NOW.

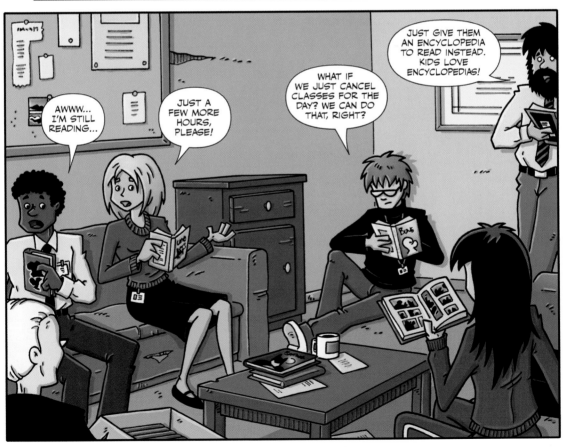

Pirate Penguin VERSUS Ninja Chicken in: Fancy Book, LEARNIN'

Mmm. Nom nom. Wasabi and Peanut Butter.

Rawr!

Surprise Swordfight!

Eek!

Aww! You made me drop my sandwich!

Oops. You made me drop my sword too.

You're just a cruddy swordsman. You have no idea how to sword fight properly, do you?

Whaddaya mean? I've got a sword, I'm fighting you. That's all you need.

I bet you don't know anything about parrying or thrusting or even the correct way to swing from chandeliers.

I am a FULLY TRAINED PIRATE, I know how to swing from a chandelier!

Prove it. Why do we have a chandelier in the kitchen?

Ernk. Gimme a boost.

Aha! Now--

Oop.

SLIP!

CRASH!

Ow.

Okay! I don't know anything about anything. Happy?

Little bit! I thought you said you knew about these things?

Actually, pirates mostly just make stuff up as they go along, it's hard training to be spontaneous. But I do have a PhD in lying.

You do?

No. That was a lie. Or was it? Mwa haha!

Wanna learn how to swordfight properly?

Nah, I was planning on watching cartoons and eating your floor sandwich.

Great! We should go find a teacher who will impart you with Knowledge Power™!

Who's Power-Tim?

141

Hello, Kung-Fu Koala's Martial Arts Academy and Chandelier Repair? Yes! I want to sign up my friend Pirate Penguin for your Advanced Fencing Class! Oh, I see.

He says Pirates are ugly and smelly and always break all the equipment, so he charges double.

Tell him I said 'So's his face!'

He says 'So's your face!' Uh-huh. He says that no, his face isn't, and that now he charges four times as much.

Well, NC, it's your money, if you want to spend 4X as much, it's up to you.

I'm not paying! They're your learning lessons, why should I pay?

Because it was my birthday last month! Besides, where are we going to find some place that gives away info for free?

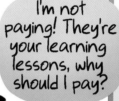

Ernest J. Bookatorium Memorial Library

Tada!

I meant TV. Like, the sword fighting channel!

That's not a real channel.

But it totally should be!

Books are better than TV anyway.

WHAT?!? I disagree entirely and challenge you to a fight to the death.

YOU DON'T KNOW HOW TO FIGHT PROPERLY. Yet. Let's go inside yonder bookatorium, and find an encyclopedia of fencing, because Knowledge is PowerTM!

Who's Power-Tim?

I'm Power Tim.

But you're a librarian.

Librarian's can be powerful.

But you're a lady. A female lady.

Female ladies can be named Tim.

But...

Shh! Btw, Mr. Penguin, here's a book on sword-fightery, complete with full-color illustrations.

Cool, look at all the blood!

How 2 STAB!

143

I also got you a handful of Moonicorn graphic novels, and a book about ice cream printed using ice cream ink.

Wow! Libraries are awesome!

Indeed! Thanks Power Tim, that was super helpful. Did you happen to find any books for me?

Um, I got you this phonebook for the city of Grumbleville, Nebraska, and a collection of Swedish rap-haikus.

Um, those seem kinda lame.

Those books are cool! It's not their fault you don't speak Swedish, or know anyone in Grumbleville.

You're weird.

That's it. You, me: It's on!

Um, can I borrow that book on fighting?

No.

THEND

BONUS LEARNING ADVENTURES!

Librarian Lady POWER TIM sez: Build your vocabulary! Circle all the words in this story you didn't understand (including the made up ones) and go look them up in the dictionary! It's like a scavenger hunt! It's fun! Kinda!

PIRATE PENGUIN Sez: Go find a book on how to make your own pirate hat, then, make one! Go go go!

NINJA CHICKEN Sez: Ninjas are so sneaky, that this activity is hiding. If you can find it, you get 20 bonus ninja points.

The moral of this story is: don't throw books at people, they don't like it.

Also, only swing from chandeliers if you're a fully trained pirate.

Also also, don't lick library books. Unless they're printed with ice cream ink.

Visual Cues

WRITTEN BY DAVID FAROZ PRECHT
ART BY CHO YOUN CHUL

WE MOVED TO SEOUL IN NOVEMBER AFTER GETTING MARRIED IN AUGUST.

MY WIFE, LINDSAY, GOT A JOB TEACHING ENGLISH AT A PRIVATE SCHOOL OR "HAGWAN," WITH A RECESSION GOING ON, JUMPING AT ANY JOB ANYWHERE, SEEMED LIKE A GOOD PLAN.

LONDON AND NEW YORK WERE SPRAWLING, BUT THEY DIDN'T BEGIN TO COMPARE TO THE DENSELY PACKED STREETS AND ALLEYS OF SEOUL. WHEN YOU DON'T KNOW THE CULTURE OR LANGUAGE, IT'S EASY TO GET LOST.

WOAH...

WE LEARNED TO LOOK FOR VISUAL CUES.

I HAD BEEN OFFERED THE CHANCE TO WRITE A STORY FOR THIS ANTHOLOGY THE WEEK BEFORE LINDSAY AND I ARRIVED IN SEOUL.

A STORY ABOUT VISUAL COMMUNICATION WOULD HAVE TO BE VISUAL, I THOUGHT.

A story about visual communication would have to be visual, I thought. The images would have to carry the text, not the other way around. |

I WANTED TO WRITE ABOUT OUR EXPERIENCES IN KOREA.

THE IMAGES WOULD HAVE TO CARRY THE TEXT, NOT THE OTHER WAY AROUND.

LINDSAY ASKED HER COLLEGE FRIEND INHAN, WHO IS KOREAN, FOR HELP FINDING AN ARTIST. INHAN FOUND CHO YOUN CHUL, A FORMER ANIMATOR LOOKING TO WORK IN COMICS.

UNFORTUNATELY, CHO'S ENGLISH WAS ONLY SLIGHTLY BETTER THAN MY KOREAN.

IS THIS SOY SAUCE OR OYSTER SAUCE?

WHAT? NO. TALKING TO MYSELF. I WANT... EUROPEAN STYLE FOR THE PANELS.

RIGHT, THE EUROPEAN KIND.

NO, NOT IN THE PANELS.

COMPLEX, DETAILED DRAWINGS... YES...WHAT?

OKAY...OKAY, WE WILL TALK WHEN WE MEET. YEAH.

IT BECAME CLEAR THAT OUR MEETINGS WOULD HAVE TO BE ONE PART ENGLISH LESSON. SPEAKING OF WHICH...

LINDSAY'S MOM WORKS AS AN ESL–OR ENGLISH AS A SECOND LANGUAGE–TEACHER IN DENVER.

GAME TIME, QUIET PLEASE!

ROCK, SCISSOR, PAPER.

ONE MINUS ONE.

SHE EXPLAINED THERE WERE TWO KEYS TO KEEPING KINDERGARTNERS FOCUSED.

GAMES AND PICTURES, AND IF YOU CAN PUT THEM TOGETHER, YOU'VE SUCCEEDED.

OKAY, PHILLIP. WHAT IS IT?

TRUCK!

GOOD. WHICH WORD IS "TRUCK"?

이번 토익 시험 잘 봤어?

....뭐 그냥 그랬어. 너는?

ONE DAY, LINDSAY TOLD ME THAT SHE WANTED TO GO BACK TO SCHOOL TO STUDY DESIGN.

SHE WAS FASCINATED BY SEOUL'S BEAUTIFUL YET SIMPLE SIGNAGE.

NOT LIKE WHAT YOU'D SEE IN MY HOMETOWN OF CHICAGO – WITH ITS EMPHASIS ON WORDS OVER PICTURES.

SHE BEGAN LOOKING AT GRAD SCHOOLS IN SEOUL.

Dong Dong Dong

BUT SHE'D NEED TO LEARN KOREAN FIRST.

TOKI.

RIGHT, AND THIS ONE?

KOREAN IS BASED ON AN ALPHABET OF 24 LETTERS.

WHAT DOES THAT SIGN SAY?

THE WRITTEN KOREAN LANGUAGE WAS CREATED TO LOOK LIKE THE SHAPES YOUR TONGUE AND MOUTH MAKE AS YOU PRONOUNCE KOREAN WORDS.

호랑이

HO-DO-RI.

HODORI!

WHILE LINDSAY LEARNED KOREAN, CHO AND I WERE TRYING TO COMMUNICATE IN HIS LIMITED ENGLISH.

LIKE THIS...

WE USED A FEATURE ON MOST NEW KOREAN CELLPHONES: THE KOREAN TO ENGLISH TRANSLATOR.

IT IS DIFFIICULT TO TYPE IN ENGLISH.

street view

AND I TRIED MY UNSKILLED HAND AT DRAWING.

OFTEN IT TOOK SOME ACTING TO GET MY POINT ACROSS.

I USED GESTURES, POINTED, OR NODDED. AND SMILED AS MUCH AS POSSIBLE.

WOW. THIS LOOKS GORGEOUS.

BECAUSE IT'S THOSE VISUAL THINGS-UNIVERSAL CUES-THAT EVERYONE, EVERYWHERE UNDERSTANDS.

YES, PERFECT, SEAH. YOU GET A STAR.

WAIT UNTIL I CALL ON YOU, PLEASE. SIT NICELY.

ALL RIGHT. COME ON UP.

ALL RIGHT, JAMES, DRAW A LINE TO "CLOCK".

Butterfly

Sheep

SEAH
JAMES
PHILLIP
DAVID
ZHONCE

PEOPLE SAY MATH IS THE UNIVERSAL LANGUAGE. I SAY IT'S VISUALS—PICTURES.

THAT IS AWESOME.

WOW... GOOD?

KEEPING YOUR MIND OPEN TO VISUAL CUES, TO THE WORLD AROUND YOU...

...SHRINKS THE WORLD. MAKES IT MORE MANAGEABLE.

LIKE A VISUAL WORLD SHOULD BE.

SEEING.

UNDERSTANDING.

The Whiteboard

a cartoon poem

Harold Buchholz

My heart skips a beat
as I rise from my seat.
I'm among the elite
who get
      to write
            on the whiteboard!

From my rear desk I go,
moving past Jen,
            then Joe,

...is Miss Hooper my foe?
Only she's
between me
and that whiteboard!

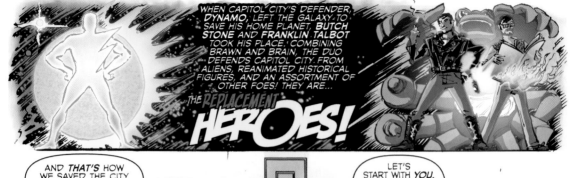

WHEN CAPITOL CITY'S DEFENDER, *DYNAMO*, LEFT THE GALAXY TO SAVE HIS HOME PLANET, *BUTCH STONE* AND *FRANKLIN TALBOT* TOOK HIS PLACE. COMBINING BRAWN AND BRAIN, THE DUO DEFENDS CAPITOL CITY FROM ALIENS, REANIMATED HISTORICAL FIGURES, AND AN ASSORTMENT OF OTHER FOES! THEY ARE...

THE REPLACEMENT HEROES!

AND *THAT'S* HOW WE SAVED THE CITY FROM TIME-TRAVELING *CONQUISTADORS*.

NOW, SINCE WE ONLY HAVE A *FEW* MINUTES LEFT, LET'S OPEN THINGS UP FOR SOME *AUDIENCE* QUESTIONS.

LET'S START WITH *YOU*. YEAH, YOU, THE POINDEXTER IN THE *THIRD* ROW.

MR. TALBOT, AS A MAN OF *SCIENCE*, WHAT MADE YOU DECIDE TO BECOME A *HERO*?

WELL, *HERO*... I DON'T KNOW THAT I'D SAY *THAT*. I MEAN--

SAME REASON I DID: *CHICKS*.

HAHA... *GOOD* ONE. *Uh*, WHAT BUTCH *MEANT* TO SAY IS THAT WHEN *DYNAMO* LEFT, CAPITOL CITY NEEDED *PROTECTORS*.

SO HERE *WE* ARE.

THAT'S WHAT CIVIC RESPONSIBILITY *IS*-- STEPPING UP AND DOING *YOUR* PART.

YOU CAN'T SIT IDLY BY AND HOPE SOMEONE *ELSE* WILL COME ALONG AND *FIX* YOUR PROBLEMS.

DON'T *WAIT* FOR A HERO-- *BE* A HERO.

WHAT WE SEEM TO HAVE ON OUR HANDS IS A SNAIL/SQUID *HYBRID.*

SINCE IT'S A SNAIL, WHAT WE NEED IS A *COMPOUND* THAT CAN--

NaCl! *SALT!* THAT WILL CAUSE HIM TO *SHRIVEL,* RIGHT?

Oh, MAKE A NITRATE COMPOUND! THAT'LL WORK BETTER THAN CHLORIDE.

NITRATE... *huh.* THAT'S AN *EXCELLENT* IDEA.

GOOD WORK!

KIDS, *DON'T* TRY THIS AT HOME...

GEEZ, HOLD ON!

FCHS PRESENTS JULES + REILLY IN

FINAL(S) CRISIS!

CREATED BY DELSANTE AND FREIRE

JULES! YOU GOTTA HELP ME! IT'S A MATTER OF LIFE OR DEATH!

CALM DOWN! WHAT IS IT?

I DIDN'T STUDY FOR MS. DUMBLETON'S FINAL!

LIGHT'S SPEED

KEVIN LaPORTE
STORY & LETTERS
AMANDA RACHELS
ART & COLORS
AMY RACHELS
COLOR ASSISTS

And this, kids, is our *biggest* and most *powerful* telescope here at the observatory.

Though as veterans of the Junior Astronomers Club, you guys probably knew that already.

This baby helps us see stars and events *so far way* that it takes millions — or even *billions* — of years for their light to reach Earth.

So, by the time we can see them, they're already *that* old!

Remember that, because I have a view of a *rare* and *beautiful* phenomenon for you winners of the "Why I Love Astronomy" essay contest.

Glen, you won *top* prize, so you're up *first*.

Hear *that*, Polly? *TOP PRIZE!*

HMPH!

Get ready to see something *truly* special!

"A red giant star in its last days before *exploding* in a supernova!"

"*SUH-WEET!*"

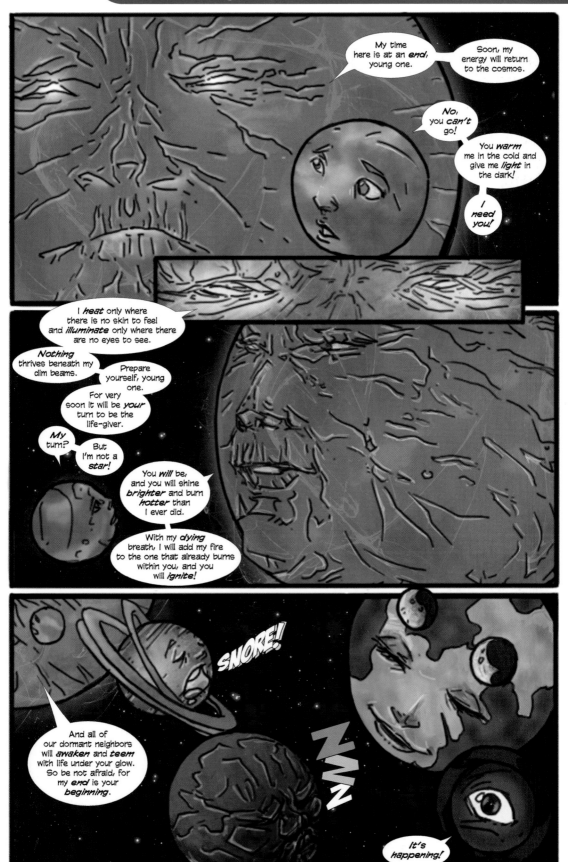

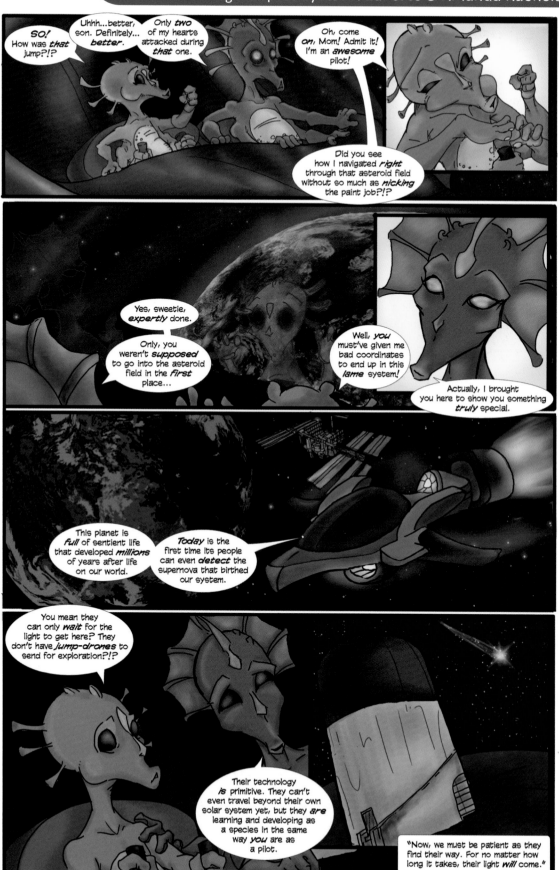

PANDORA
CELEBRITY SUPERHEROINE
In "Asking the Right Questions"
story: Josh Elder   art: Jen Brazas   letters: Steve Wallace

Pandora is the most famous 16-year-old on the planet. She's on the cover of every magazine and gets invited to all the best parties. Oh, and she's also a superhero. You know, in her spare time...

"YESTERDAY WE DISCUSSED HOW TO SAFELY STOP A RUNAWAY TRAIN..."

...THROUGH THE PROPER APPLICATION OF NEWTON'S LAWS OF MOTION.

...will stay in motion until acted upon

$f=ma$

TODAY I AM GOING TO TEACH YOU ABOUT FARADAY'S THEORY OF ELECTROMAGNETIC INDUCTION AND HOW IT CAN BE USED TO HELP YOU DEAL WITH TECHNOLOGY-BASED THREATS.

PROFESSOTRON
Origin: Advanced artificial intelligence
Powers: Digital Intellect
Hobbies: Chess, Astrophysics and Swing Dancing

THE ENEMY

AND AT THE RISK OF SOUNDING IMMODEST, YOU CARBON-BASED LIFEFORMS NEED ALL THE HELP YOU CAN GET.

AS THE TERM "ELECTROMAGNETISM" IMPLIES, AN ELECTRIC CHARGE GENERATES A MAGNETIC FIELD AND VICE VERSA.

SUFFICIENTLY POWERFUL BURSTS OF ELECTROMAGNETIC RADIATION LIKE A BOLT OF LIGHTNING, A NUCLEAR EXPLOSION OR A SOLAR FLARE CAN GENERATE A POWERFUL PULSE OF ELECTROMAGNETIC ENERGY.

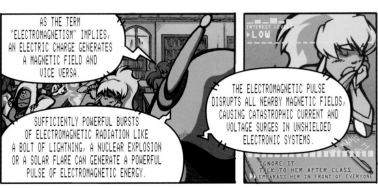

INTEREST LEVEL
► LOW

THE ELECTROMAGNETIC PULSE DISRUPTS ALL NEARBY MAGNETIC FIELDS, CAUSING CATASTROPHIC CURRENT AND VOLTAGE SURGES IN UNSHIELDED ELECTRONIC SYSTEMS.

IGNORE IT
TALK TO HER AFTER CLASS
EMBARASS HER IN FRONT OF EVERYONE

Am I boring you, Pandora?

PANDORA PERFECT
Origin: Daughter of the science-enhanced Prometheus Perfect and the magic-empowered Lady Valkyrie
Powers: Flight, Superstrength, Superspeed, Invulnerability and the ability to properly Accessorize any outfit
Personality: A little flighty, but her heart is in the right place

BUSTED!

NO! I MEAN, WELL... KIND OF.

I JUST DON'T GET HOW ALL THIS SCIENCE STUFF IS GOING TO HELP US IN THE *REAL WORLD* OF SUPERVILLAINS AND GIANT, RADIOACTIVE MONSTERS.

ALPHA MALE
Origin: Genetically engineered (and ginormously entitled) optimal human
Powers: Highly-trained Martial Artist and superb Smacktalker
Team Affiliation: The A-List

YEAH, AND IF YOU GOT A *ROBOT* PROBLEM YOU JUST FIND THE POINDEXTER WHO BUILT IT, AND THEN YOU HIT HIM IN THE *FACE*.

CRASH!

PROBLEM SOLVED!

I HEAR THAT!

OR YOU JUST, YOU KNOW, FIND THE *OFF SWITCH*.

Those are all very... interesting theories. You will have the opportunity to test them next period when you join Professor Praetorian for a field trip into the city.

INGÉNOVA
Origin: Intergalactic princess-in-exile from the Antares Nebula
Powers: Solar-Powered Flight and Energy Blasts
Talents: Acting, Modeling and Snobbery

B-BOY
Origin: Cybernetically augmented by his record label to be fresher, flyer, more dope
Powers: Superhuman Agility and Quickness
Debut Album: *Straight Outta Gotham* feat. Kid Awesome

Whereupon I predict you will discover that lessons learned in the classroom have more relevance to the real world than you imagine.

THE MEDIA HATH DUBBED THEM THE *8-BIT BANDITS.*

SO WHAT ARE THESE 'BOTS CALLED AGAIN?

PROFESSOR PRAETORIAN
Origin: A Roman Centurion transported through time to the modern day
Powers: Hi-Tech Armor and Weapons
Faculty Position: Personal Combat Instructor

"THEY STEAL ADVANCED TECHNOLOGICAL COMPONENTS AT THE BEHEST OF THEIR VILE CREATOR, THE VILLAINOUS **NERDCORE.**"

HOW ARE YOU GENTLEMEN?

ALL YOUR BASE...

...ARE BELONG TO US.

WHAT YOU SAY?

YOU HAVE NO CHANCE TO SURVIVE.

YOU ARE ON THE WAY TO DESTRUCTION.

MAKE YOUR TIME.

HAHAHA

'TIS THEIR THIRD SUCH ACT OF BRIGANDRY IN AS MANY WEEKS. AND BY *JUPITER,* I SWEAR 'TWILL BE THEIR LAST!

NOW TO BATTLE!

YEAH! IT IS ON!

AND REMEMBER -- YOUR PERFORMANCE THIS DAY COUNTS AS 20 PERCENT OF YOUR FINAL GRADE!

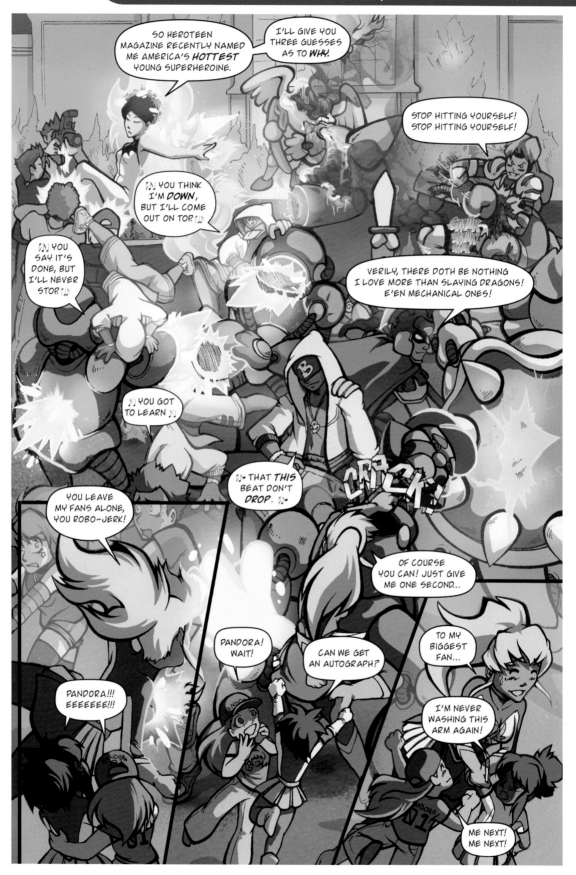

GREAT JOB, GUYS. I MEAN, YOU TOOK OUT SOME *DIY 'BOTS* I BUILT USING SPARE PARTS AND THE PROCESSORS FROM OLD *VIDEOGAME* CONSOLES. THAT'S *REALLY* IMPRESSIVE.

BUT *SPOILER ALERT*...

... MY 8-BIT BANDITS WEREN'T JUST STEALING RANDOM TECHAGE. THEY WERE GATHERING THE INGREDIENTS FOR MY MECHA MASTERPIECE.

NERDCORE
Origin: Geekery-themed villain
Powers: Mad Programming Skillz
Base of Operations: The Nerdcave (AKA his mom's basement)

YOU HEROLEBRITIES ARE SO GOING TO GET *PWNED*. BEHOLD MY GREATEST CREATION ...

MECHA-RAAAAAGGGGRRRGGHHH!

... THE **MECHANNOSAURUS REX!**

THIS IS WHY I ALWAYS SAY THAT YOU DON'T FIGHT THE ROBOT, YOU FIGHT THE **DORKIMUS MAXIMUS** WHO BUILT IT.

HOPE YOU BROUGHT SOME ASPIRIN, **NERDCLOWN**...

...'CAUSE I'M ABOUT TO BRING THE PAIN!

SPLAT!

EPIC FORCE FIELD FAIL, L053R.

THAT NERDCORE NUTCASE JUST **BLEW UP** B-BOY! I CAN'T GET BLOWN UP! DO YOU KNOW WHAT THAT WOULD DO TO MY **MODELING** CAREER?!

CALM DOWN! NO ONE (ELSE) IS GETTING BLOWN UP, OKAY?

SO LISTEN UP: THERE ARE INNOCENT PEOPLE DOWN THERE THAT NEED PROTECTING, A BAD GUY THAT NEEDS **STOPPING** AND A DAY THAT NEEDS SAVING.

YOU'RE A **SUPERHERO** — IT'S TIME TO START **ACTING** LIKE ONE!

YOU-YOU'RE RIGHT. SO WHAT DO WE DO?

WELL, REMEMBER IN CLASS TODAY WHEN PROFESSOTRON SAID THAT A **SOLAR STORM** COULD GENERATE ONE OF THESE ELECTROMAGNETIC PULSE THINGIES THAT FRY COMPUTER CHIPS AND STUFF?

UH, NO. NOT REALLY...

⁖SIGH⁖ WELL HE DID, AND SINCE YOU'RE SOLAR POWERED, YOU CAN MAKE ONE OF THOSE PULSES. SO YOU GO **NOVA**...

...AND I'LL PROVIDE THE **DISTRACTION.**

HEY RUSTY! YOUR MOTHER WAS A **DUMP TRUCK!**

CTRL-ALT-DEL!

KLANG!

OOF!

NERDCORE FTW. LOL.

YOU HAVEN'T... WON... YET...

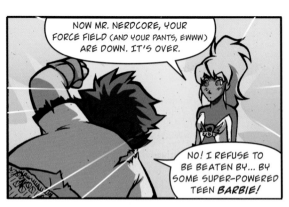

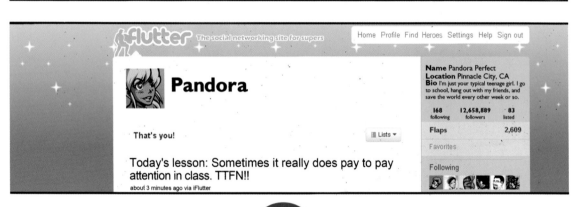

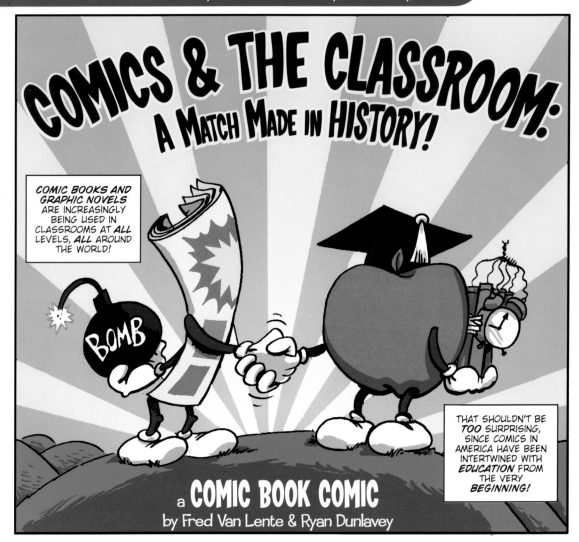

COMICS & THE CLASSROOM:
A MATCH MADE IN HISTORY!

COMIC BOOKS AND GRAPHIC NOVELS ARE INCREASINGLY BEING USED IN CLASSROOMS AT **ALL** LEVELS, **ALL** AROUND THE WORLD!

THAT SHOULDN'T BE **TOO** SURPRISING, SINCE COMICS IN AMERICA HAVE BEEN INTERTWINED WITH **EDUCATION** FROM THE VERY **BEGINNING**!

a **COMIC BOOK COMIC**
by Fred Van Lente & Ryan Dunlavey

IN FACT, THE COMIC BOOK AS WE KNOW IT WAS PRACTICALLY **INVENTED** BY AN EDUCATOR -- MAXWELL C. GAINES, A FORMER BRONX HIGH SCHOOL PRINCIPAL!

SINCE THE FIRST COMIC STRIPS APPEARED IN THE 1890S, KIDS HAD BEEN THROWING OUT EVERY **OTHER** SECTION OF THE NEWSPAPER TO GET TO THEIR BELOVED "**FUNNIES**."

BUT IT WOULDN'T BE UNTIL **1933** THAT SOMEONE HIT ON THE IDEA OF SELLING PERIODICALS THAT WERE NOTHING **BUT** COMICS DIRECTLY **TO** KIDS!

GAINES SLAPPED 10-CENT STICKERS ON **FAMOUS FUNNIES**, A PROMOTIONAL GIVEAWAY REPRINTING POPULAR STRIPS, LEFT THEM AT VARIOUS NEW YORK CITY NEWSSTANDS OVER A WEEEKEND ...

...AND WAS STUNNED TO DISCOVER THEY **SOLD OUT** BY **MONDAY!**

GAINES SOON BEGAN PRODUCING **ORIGINAL** COMIC BOOK MATERIAL. A STRIP HE BOUGHT FROM TWO RECENT HIGH SCHOOL GRADUATES IN CLEVELAND, **"SUPERMAN"** BY JERRY SIEGEL AND JERRY SHUSTER, PROVED TO BE THE MEGA-HIT THAT PUT COMICS ON THE MAP COMMERCIALLY IN 1938!

GAINES REMAINED A **TEACHER** AT HEART, THOUGH. USING THE MONEY HE MADE IN THE SUPER HERO FIELD HE FOUNDED A NEW PUBLISHER IN 1946, **EDUCATIONAL** COMICS, OR **EC.**

"I DON'T CARE **HOW** LONG IT TOOK MOSES TO CROSS THE DESERT!

"I WANT IT IN THREE PANELS!"*

* ACTUAL QUOTE!

EC'S FIRST TITLES INCLUDED *PICTURE STORIES FROM AMERICAN HISTORY* AND *PICTURE STORIES FROM THE BIBLE*, ALL PRODUCED TO MAX'S NOTORIOUSLY (COUGH) **COST-CONSCIOUS** STANDARDS...

PICTURE STORIES FROM WORLD HISTORY AND *PICTURE STORIES FROM SCIENCE* SOON FOLLOWED, BUT, ALAS, NONE SOLD VERY WELL.

THEN, TRAGICALLY, MAX AND A FRIEND WERE KILLED IN A **BOAT COLLISION** ON NEW YORK'S LAKE PLACID IN 1947.

OOPS.

MAX'S TWENTY-FIVE YEAR OLD SON **BILL** -- ABOUT TO BECOME A **CHEMISTRY TEACHER** HIMSELF -- INHERITED HIS DAD'S BUSINESS.

HE WANTED TO STAY IN **EDUCATION**, BUT HIS MOTHER **BEGGED** HIM TO TRY AND KEEP THE COMPANY AFLOAT, FOR IT WAS ALL THEY HAD LEFT OF HIS FATHER.

BILL GAINES TURNED EC AROUND BY CHANGING ITS NAME TO **ENTERTAINING** COMICS AND CRANKING OUT GORY HORROR TITLES LIKE **TALES FROM THE CRYPT** THAT SOON MADE IT FAMOUS!

UNFORTUNATELY, **TOC** AND THE OTHER EC SMASH-HIT, **MAD MAGAZINE**, DID NOTHING TO DISPEL GAINES' FELLOW TEACHERS' **SUSPICIONS** ABOUT COMICS.

AS EARLY AS 1942 HORRIFIED ARTICLES LIKE "THE PLAGUE OF THE COMICS" BEGAN APPEARING IN **ELEMENTARY ENGLISH REVIEW** AND OTHER TEACHERS' JOURNALS.

BY 1948, **BOTH** THE NATIONAL CONGRESS OF PARENTS AND THE NATIONAL EDUCATION ASSOCIATION WERE CALLING FOR **FEDERAL REGULATION** OF THE INDUSTRY!

THE HYSTERIA WAS **UNDERSTANDABLE** IN THE SENSE THAT COMIC BOOKS WERE AMONG THE FIRST MASS MEDIA TO BE MARKETED DIRECTLY **TO** CHILDREN, AS OPPOSED TO **PARENTS** TO BUY **FOR** THEIR KIDS.

AT A **DIME** A POP, KIDS COULD BUY COMICS WITH THEIR OWN MONEY AND ENJOY THEM WITHOUT A **TRACE** OF ADULT SUPERVISION.

PUBLIC ENEMY NUMBER ONE ON TEACHERS' FOUR-COLOR **HATE LIST** WAS THE COMICS SERIES THAT SWORE UP AND DOWN IT WAS THE **MOST** EDUCATIONAL...

I'D LIKE TO REGALE THE CLASS, MRS. HODGKISS, WITH MY BOOK REPORT ON **REMEMBRANCE OF THINGS PAST**...

WAIT A...

...DID YOU READ THE **BOOK**, OR THE **CLASSICS ILLUSTRATED** VERSION?!

CLASSICS ILLUSTRATED WAS FOUNDED IN 1941* BY ALBERT LEWIS KANTER, A RUSSIAN IMMIGRANT WHO HAD PREVIOUSLY CREATED A **TOY TELEGRAPH**.

HMMM...MY **THREE MUSKETEERS** IN **MORSE CODE** ISN'T REALLY COMING ACROSS...

I KNOW! I'LL TRY **COMICS**!

THEIR COMIC BOOK ADAPTATIONS OF CLASSIC WORKS OF LITERATURE LIKE **ROBINSON CRUSOE, MACBETH,** AND **GULLIVER'S TRAVELS** PROVED **SO** IMMENSELY POPULAR...

ORIGINALLY CLASSICS **COMICS**; THE NAME CHANGED IN **1947**, PROBABLY TO AVOID ADULTS' GROWING OUTCRY AGAINST ALL THINGS COMICS-Y.

...THAT THEY WENT THROUGH MULTIPLE **REPRINTINGS** (UNHEARD OF FOR COMICS IN THOSE DAYS) AND ALLOWED KIDS IN **TWO DOZEN** COUNTRIES TO CHEAT ON BOOK REPORTS IN **NINE LANGUAGES!**

ME GUSTA REGALAR A SU CLASE, SRA. HODGKISS, CON MI REPORTE DE LIBRE ACERCA DE *EN BUSCA DEL TIEMPO PERDIDO...*

ESPERA UN...

WHEN THE OUTCRY FROM PARENTS AND TEACHERS FORCED THE INDUSTRY TO REGULATE ITSELF WITH THE 1955 **COMICS CODE AUTHORITY**, CLASSICS ILLUSTRATED **REFUSED** TO CARRY THE CCA SEAL, CLAIMING THEY HELD THEMSELVES TO HIGHER LITERARY STANDARDS THAN THE CODE DEMANDED ANYWAY!

YOU WOULDN'T DARE **CENSOR** THE BARD OF **AVON**, WOULD YOU?

NAW, SO LONG AS YOU DON'T HAVE THE **MURDER**, INCEST, TORTURE AND **WITCHCRAFT** THE CODE PROHIBITS!

APPROVED BY THE COMICS CODE **A** AUTHORITY

UM... NO, OF **COURSE** NOT, DON'T BE **SILLY...** ~HEH!~

"IN A WORLD OF **BAD** COMICS, WE WERE THE **BEST,**" SNIFFED *CLASSICS* EDITOR AND WRITER MEYER KAPLIN.

"WE WERE THE **CLEANEST**, WE WERE THE MOST **RESEARCHED**, AND, WITHIN THE LIMITATIONS OF OUR PAGE LENGTH, AS **FAITHFUL** TO THE ORIGINAL AS HUMANLY POSSIBLE."

THOUGH REDUCING 400- AND 500-PAGE PROSE NOVELS TO, ON AVERAGE, **48 PAGES** OF COMIC BOOK MEANT A CERTAIN AMOUNT OF MATERIAL HAD TO BE... **TRUNCATED...**

ALL KIDDING ASIDE, *CLASSICS ILLUSTRATED* CAN BE CREDITED WITH AWAKENING A LOVE OF LITERATURE IN **MILLIONS** OF KIDS.

CIRCULATION PEAKED IN 1960, WHEN THE AVERAGE ADAPTATION ENJOYED A PRINT RUN OF **262,000 COPIES.**

BUT NEW TITLES STOPPED APPEARING IN **1962**, DONE IN LARGELY BY COMPETITION FROM *CLIFF'S NOTES*, WHICH DEBUTED IN 1958.

HOMER'S **THE ODYSSEY** (IN ONE PANEL)

HONEY, I'M HOME!

WELL *THAT* WAS QUICK...

I'M SO MUCH MORE "LITERARCILY" THAN THOSE STUPID **COMICS**, RIGHT?

CLIFF

THAT *IS* HOW YOU SAY THAT, RIGHT...?

NOOOOOO!!

THE *U.S. MILITARY* FIRST PIONEERED THE USE OF COMICS AS AN ACTUAL *TEACHING TOOL*, THANKS PRIMARILY TO CARTOONIST *WILL EISNER*, WHO WOUND UP AT THE ORDNANCE DEPARTMENT'S *ABERDEEN PROVING GROUND* IN MARYLAND AFTER HE WAS DRAFTED INTO WORLD WAR TWO.

EISNER'S WEEKLY NEWSPAPER COMIC BOOK *THE SPIRIT* WAS A POPULAR FEATURE IN THE NEARBY *BALTIMORE SUN*; THE BRASS QUICKLY RECOGNIZED WILL AND MADE HIM ART DIRECTOR OF THE SERVICE MAGAZINE *ARMY MOTORS*.

ARMY MOTORS WAS A KEY PART OF ORDNANCE'S ON-GOING EFFORTS TO INURE THE CONCEPT OF *PREVENTIVE* MAINTENANCE INTO THE G.I. -- THE IDEA THAT KEEPING ONE'S WEAPONS AND EQUIPMENT IN GOOD CONDITION *BEFORE* THEY BROKE WAS MOST EFFICIENT *AND* SAFEST.

1 Manually unfasten and vertically depress lower extremity-covering clothing; THEN

2 Place cover into second, or ascendant, position; THEN

3 Turn body so face and genital area face away from stool-receiving device; THEN

4 Affix gluteus maximus to aperture so sphincter is directly over water basin; THEN

BUT, *PRE*-EISNER, IT WAS, LIKE MOST ARMY PUBLICATIONS, ANTISEPTIC, JARGON-RIDDEN AND *BORING*.

EISNER CONVINCED HIS SUPERIORS TO LET HIM USE *COMICS* TO TEACH PREVENTIVE MAINTENANCE WITH HUMOR AND PLAIN LANGUAGE, THEREBY IMPROVING SOLDIERS' COMPREHENSION AND *RETENTION*.

UP UNTIL THIS POINT, THE MILITARY HAD DEEMED COMICS FIT ONLY FOR *PROPAGANDA*-- SUCH AS *"HOW TO SPOT A JAP,"* WHICH THE ARMY COMMISSIONED FROM *TERRY AND THE PIRATES* CARTOONIST *MILTON CANIFF*.

"How to Spot a Jap"

Evil thoughts

Baby-eating teeth

Freedom-hating finger-nails

PREDICTABLY, EISNER RAN UP AGAINST THE HIGHER-UPS' RESISTANCE TO *ANYTHING* THAT DEVIATED FROM PREVIOUSLY ESTABLISHED PROCEDURE.

WHAT *IS* THIS *POPPYCOCK?* ACCIDENT PREVENTION IS *SERIOUS* BUSINESS! YOU CAN'T USE *SILLY DRAWINGS* TO PROMOTE IT!

AND EVEN *WORSE* -- IN YOUR STRIPS YOU *MOCK* SUPERIOR OFFICERS BY INSINUATING *WE DON'T KNOW WHAT WE'RE TALKING ABOUT!!!*

AS IF VOLUNTEERING TO PROVE WILL'S POINT, THE ADJUTANT GENERAL IN CHARGE OF PRODUCING *TECHNICAL MATERIALS* ARRANGED FOR THE *UNIVERSITY OF CHICAGO* TO RUN AN *EFFICIENCY TEST* PITTING STANDARD MANUALS AGAINST EISNER'S *COMICS*...AND THE *COMICS* WON *HANDILY!*

with comics

without comics

Who is on *first!*

I'm asking *you* who's on first!

That's the man's name.

That's who's name? Right.

Look. You got a first baseman?

Certainly.

Who's on first? That's right.

When you pay the first baseman every month, who gets the money?

Every penny.

AAAAAAAAAAA RRRRRRRRRRR GGGGGGGGGGG!!

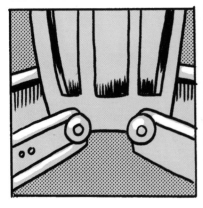  

AS HIS BIOGRAPHER BOB ANDELMAN WRITES,
"THE RESULTS *REINFORCED* WHAT EISNER BELIEVED TO BE *CHARACTERISTIC* OF THE COMIC STRIP: "THE *EASE* WITH WHICH *IMAGES* DEMONSTRATED *PROCESS.*"

THE SAME SEQUENTIAL PROCESS THAT COULD EXPERTLY RENDER THE BACK-AND-FORTH OF A *VAUDEVILLE COMEDY ROUTINE* IN THE *NEWSPAPER FUNNIES* ALLOWED EISNER TO DEMONSTRATE A TECHNICALLY *COMPLEX* TASK -- SUCH AS REMOVING *VOLUTE SPRINGS* FROM A *TANK* -- FROM THE POINT OF VIEW OF THE *REPAIRMAN.* COMIC ART DRAWS THE READER *INTO* THE SEQUENCE, MAKES HER A *PART* OF IT, STEP BY STEP!

ARMY MOTORS AND ITS SUCCESSOR, *P*S: THE PREVENTIVE MAINTENANCE MONTHLY*, PROVED *SO* SUCCESSFUL AT EDUCATING SOLDIERS AND OFFICERS THAT EISNER REMAINED ITS ART DIRECTOR LONG AFTER HE MUSTERED OUT!

SO HE COULD KEEP UP-TO-DATE ON THE LATEST EQUIPMENT AND TECHNIQUES, THE MILITARY SENT EISNER ON TOURS OF ARMY POSTINGS AROUND THE WORLD -- INCLUDING HOTSPOTS LIKE THE *KOREAN DMZ* AND *SAIGON*, WHERE HE GOT *GLOWING REVIEWS* FROM THE SOLDIERS THEMSELVES!

HIS INSPIRATION CAME IN THE FORM OF DARKEST *TRAGEDY*.

IN 1969, EISNER'S BELOVED TEENAGE DAUGHTER ALICE HAD SUCCUMBED TO *LEUKEMIA*.

THE ARTIST POURED HIS GRIEF AND RAGE INTO A SHORT COMICS STORY, *"A CONTRACT WITH GOD,"* ABOUT A DEPRESSION-ERA HASSIDIC JEW WHO REJECTS HIS FAITH WHEN HIS DAUGHTER DIES UNEXPECTEDLY.

"YOU THE GUY WHO DOES THOSE *PICTURES?*"

"YEAH..."

"MAN, YOU SAVED MY @$$, YOU KNOW THAT?"*

* ACTUAL EXCHANGE!

WHEN EISNER FINALLY GAVE UP HIS LUCRATIVE ARMY CONTRACT IN *1971*, HIS WIFE ANN ENCOURAGED HIM TO TAKE THE NEXT BIG LEAP AND CREATE A COMIC AIMED AT *ADULTS*, WITH ADULT THEMES.

EISNER COMBINED THAT TALE WITH THREE OTHERS ABOUT 1930'S JEWS IN HIS NATIVE BRONX, CALLING THE COLLECTION *A CONTRACT WITH GOD AND OTHER TENEMENT STORIES.*

HE FELT WEIGHTY MATERIAL SUCH AS THIS DEMANDED TO BE PUBLISHED AND DISTRIBUTED BY A MAINSTREAM (I.E., *NON-COMICS*) PUBLISHER, BUT STRUGGLED OVER A WAY TO *MARKET* THE UNIQUE PROJECT.

THOUGH EISNER DIDN'T ORIGINATE THE TERM *"GRAPHIC NOVEL,"* ITS APPEARANCE ON THE TRADE PAPERBACK COVER OF *A CONTRACT WITH GOD* (1978) BROUGHT IT INTO *POPULAR USAGE* FOR THE FIRST TIME.

THROUGH RACKED IN *BOOKSTORES* AS ITS AUTHOR INTENDED, BAFFLED CLERKS DIDN'T KNOW WHETHER TO SHELVE *CONTRACT* IN THE "RELIGION" OR "HUMOR" SECTIONS... AS OPPOSED TO *"FICTION,"* WHERE IT RIGHTLY BELONGED!

IT'S...A...UH..."GRAPHIC" ER...AH..."NOVEL!"

YEAH, THAT'S THE TICKET!

"OH, THAT SOUNDS INTERESTING; I'VE NEVER *HEARD* OF THAT BEFORE."

THIS "COMIC" HAS *NAKED LADIES* AND *BAD WORDS* IN IT! WHAT IS IT DOING NEXT TO MY PRECIOUS, PRECIOUS *GARFIELD?!*

MISTER SIMMONS! HAAAALP!!

OY!

SINCE EISNER'S BOLD EXPERIMENT, IT'S THE MORE SOPHISTICATED LITERARY ASPIRATIONS OF "GRAPHIC NOVELS" (REALLY JUST A SYNONYM FOR *"LONG COMIC BOOK"*) THAT HAVE LED THEM TO BE USED IN THE CLASSROOM AT EVERY LEVEL!

PRE-READERS USE *WORDLESS* GRAPHIC NOVELS TO IMPROVE *VERBAL NARRATIVE SKILLS!*

YOU TELL *ME* THE STORY...

OKAY... WELL... THE GIRL AND HER DOG ARE GOING UP THE HILL...

GOOD! AND WHAT HAPPENS *NEXT...?*

KORGI

WE *THINK VISUALLY.* AS WILL EISNER DISCOVERED WITH HIS ARMY MANUALS, COMICS *REINFORCE* PROCESS, AS IN THE DECODING OF SYMBOLS REQUIRED FOR LITERACY...

R-A-T-T-H-I-N-G...

...AS WELL AS MORE EASILY CONVEY *ABSTRACT CONCEPTS*, NOT UNLIKE HOW *POLITICAL CARTOONISTS* SATIRIZE THE ISSUES OF THE DAY IN THE NEWSPAPER!

PLATO'S *THEORY OF FORMS...* IT'S KIND OF LIKE A *MOVIE THEATER!*

I THINK I *GOT* IT, NOW!

ACTION PHICOS

AND *MOST* IMPORTANTLY, COMICS ARE NOW BEING TAUGHT NOT AS *CLASSICS*-STYLE ADAPTATIONS, BUT VALUABLE WORKS OF LITERATURE WITH THEIR *OWN* INTRINSIC MERIT!

FUTURE GENERATIONS OF TEACHERS WILL DECIDE HOW BEST TO USE COMICS AND GRAPHIC NOVELS IN THEIR CLASSES -- STARTING *HERE AND NOW!*

PERSEPOLIS

Honor Roll

The Honor Roll is our way of recognizing the extraordinary people, companies and comic specialty retailers that have gone above and beyond in their support of our mission to revolutionize the role of comics in the classroom. (illustrations by Lin Workman)

Becky Conzett

Josh Hime

Peter Gutiérrez

Robert Jarosinski

Russ Burlingame

Brett Schenker

Liza Illuzzi

DONOR APPEARANCES

The following donors to Reading With Pictures were awarded cameo appearances in select stories as a way of giving thanks for their support.

Perry Beckett in *G-Man: Reign of the Robo-Teachers*, Brian Bontemps in *Light's Speed*, Kimberly Campbell in *So Much More*, Kathleen Dolan in *High Noon at Junior High*, Ms. Dumbleton in *FCHS: Final(s) Crisis!*, Mitch Dyer in *G-Man*, Martin Fung in *Albert the Alien is New in School*, Jason W. Gavin in *G-Man*, Charlotte Johnson in *Just James and the Playground of the Living Dead*, Jack Hayes in *G-Man*, Charles Henry in *G-Man*, Noah Henry in *G-Man*, Donald Higgins in *Pandora: Celebrity Superheroine*, Adkins P. Jones in *Light's Speed*, Mariel Saginaw in *Just James*, Kristen Whitaker in *Heroes*, Jennifer Reall in *G-Man*, and Lee-Anne Weber in *G-Man*

Honor Roll

Bitstrips for Schools
www.bitstripsforschools.com

Casablanca Comics
Portland, ME

Challengers Comics + Conversation
Chicago, IL

Chapel Hill Comics
Chapel Hill, NC

Chicago Comics
Chicago, IL

The Comic Vault
Chicago, IL

Comix Revolution
Evanston, IL
Mt. Prospect, IL

Jim Hanley's Universe
New York, NY

Spotlight
www.abdopublishing.com

Tokyopop
www.tokyopop.com

Westfield
www.westfieldcomics.com

Contributors

Jason Allen (*Just James*): Jason Allen is co-creator and illustrator of *Just James and The Playground of the Living Dead*. A corn-fed Midwesterner, Jason relocated to the deep south in 2005. While adding "y'all" to his vernacular, he has illustrated characters and props on the television shows *Frisky Dingo* and *Archer*. His eclectic background also includes theatrical design, voiceovers, and Karaoke DJ-ing. His Piano Man rocks! Check out his website at www.jasondallen.com.

Gene Ambaum (*Unshelved*): Gene is the writer of *Unshelved* and editor of the Unshelved Book Club. He uses a pen name because he is scared of his own shadow. He has worked a variety of jobs in public libraries in the Pacific Northwest, including teen services and staff training. He loves French graphic novels, television shows from his childhood, pina coladas, and getting caught in the rain. www.unshelved.com

Bill Barnes (*Unshelved*): Bill is the artist of Unshelved and writer of *Not Invented Here*. Before taking the vow of poverty required of cartoonists, Bill worked in the software industry for twenty years as a programmer, user interface designer, and executive speechwriter. He is teaching himself to play ukulele. Born in Manhattan, Bill is now a naturalized citizen of Seattle. www.unshelved.com

Gabriel Bautista (*Albert the Alien*): Gabriel is an indy comic artist, and an Eisner award winning colorist. His work can been seen in Image's *Popgun VOL 2* and *Elephantmen*. His coloring work can be seen in DC Comics' *The Spirit*. Follow his adventures at http://galvomode.com!!

Chris Beckett (*Mail Order Ninja, The Replacement Heroes*) is a comic colorist residing in Brooklyn. His favorite color is salmon, which also happens to be his third favorite freshwater fish. His least favorite color is camel, which weirdly enough is his favorite even-toed ungulate.

John Bivens (*What if Mr. Kilsome Was a Monster?*): John recently graduated from Northern Illinois University. Since that time he has done work for Sam Costello's *Split Lip* horror anthology, *Comic Book Tattoo* (the Tori Amos-based anthology), Popgun volume 4, and has appeared in a handful of Zuda web-comic competitions. He spends whatever spare time he can with his lovely fiancée Mallory.

Phillip Bowles (*Stellar Rescue!*): Phillip discovered comic books at the tender age of six, the first being *Robocop #1* from a local 7-Eleven. It was clearly love at first sight. Since then, Phillip has pursued a career as a comics artist and continues to do so as a student in the Illustration As Visual Essay Masters program at the School of Visual Arts, NYC. Examples of his work can be found at www.phillipbowles.com

Michael Vincent Bramley (*Judgment of Patrick*): Michael has been a fan of comics from a young age. Teachers would reprimand him for trying to read comics during quiet time, or drawing monsters and writing stories about them in the margins of his school notebooks. Nowadays Michael lives in NYC with his wife, Alice, and spends all day making things up for his webcomic, *Hadron Colliderscope*.

Jen Brazas (*Pandora*): Jennifer Brazas is actually a ninja. But sadly, ninjas are not a recession-proof profession, so she turned to making comics. With her amazing ninja powers, she's able to churn out hilarious full-color comic pages twice-weekly (Mondays and Fridays) of her webcomic *Mystic Revolution*, which can be found at www.mysticrev.com. *Mystic Revolution* currently has two self-published graphic novels with a third one set for release in Summer 2010.

Ed Brisson (*Overdue*): Ed is a freelance comic book letterer and writer. Since 2005, he's been running the small publishing outfit New Reliable Press. He currently lives in Vancouver with his wife, daughter and their menagerie of pets. Find him online at edbrisson.com.

Jeffrey Brown (*Little Bighead and the Big Snow*): Jeffrey Brown is best known for his autobiographical graphic novels like *Clumsy* and *Funny Misshapen Body*, as well as humorous work Incredible *Change-Bots*, *Cats Are Weird*, and *Bighead*. He lives in Chicago with his wife and son. www.topshelfcomix.com/catalog/jeffrey-brown

Harold Buchholz (*The Whiteboard*): Harold is helping revitalize the children's comics field as a publishing consultant, working with companies such as Archie Comics and Renaissance Press. Over the years he has helped hundreds of cartoonists get their work in print. In 2010 he received a Gold Pixie award for outstanding 2D animation. Find him online at www.acredale.com

Dino Caruso (*Overdue*): Dino Caruso hails from Ontario, Canada, where he lives with his wife and son. He has self-published a few comics, notably *Against the Wall* and *Olga*. He's been published in a variety of anthologies from publishers including Ape Entertainment, Heske Horror and Poseur Ink. Check out his website at http://www.carusocomics.com

Phil Chan (*Dr. Stevelove*): For as long as he can remember, Phil Chan has always wanted to create comics. He eventually found himself on the new frontier of webcomics, co-creating and writing the college-themed comic *Matriculated*. More recently, he also co-created and wrote the hybrid video game comic/review column *Another Videogame Webcomic*. Phil currently resides in Delaware, where he enjoys tax-free shopping and fight clubs.

Cho Youn Chul (*Visual Cues*) was born and raised in Seoul, South Korea and has a degree in animation from Sejong University. His English is not that bad, despite what his English grade says. But that's okay; he doesn't have to worry about grades anymore. He works at Dot & Comma Communication studio.

Scott Cunningham (*A Misguided Field Guide*) is co-creator of *Lil' Bigfoot* (lilbigfoot.com), the smelly, hairy hominid who stars in his RWP story, and who originally stunk up the pages of *Nickelodeon Magazine*. Scott's work has also appeared in *Heavy Metal*, *Mad*, *Mad Kids*, *Archie*, and a slew of DC comics, including their Kids' Line titles and Vertigo. Some of his recent stories are featured in DC's Cartoon Network 2-1 Anthology released this summer.

Vito Delsante (*FCHS: Final(s) Crisis!*): Vito is a writer. He's written for DC Comics, Marvel Comics, Dynamite Entertainment, AdHouse Books, and Simon & Schuster, among others and his stories have been reprinted in other countries. He and Rachel Freire have self-published FCHS and it is available online. He lives in New York City with his wife, Michelle, and two dogs, and wears glasses. Visit him online at www.incogvito.com.

Ryan Dunlavey (*Comics & the Classroom*): Ryan is best known as the artist and co-creator of the American Library Award winning *Action Philosophers* comic book series (with author Fred Van Lente). Some of Ryan's other comics include *Modok* for Marvel Comics and the self-published *Comic Book Comics* (also with Van Lente), the first cartoon history of the American comic book industry. His work has appeared in *Mad*, *Wizard*, *ToyFare*, *The Princeton Review*, *Time Out* and *Disney Adventures*. He lives in New York City with his wife and son.

Joe Dunn (*Dr. Stevelove*): While obtaining a degree from Parsons School of Design Joe Dunn fell in love; first with sequential storytelling and then with a lady. He's spent the last decade devoted to those two things, tying the knot and working steadily in illustration and webcomics. Joe's since relocated from the big bad city to the peaceful suburbs of NJ, where he hopes that his odd hours and rowdy music don't bother the neighbors.

Josh Elder (Editor, *Pandora*, *Mail Order Ninja*, *Just James*): Josh is the founder and Executive Director of Reading With Pictures. Creator of the award-winning graphic novel series and nationally syndicated comic strip *Mail Order Ninja*, Josh regularly hosts workshops and professional development seminars in schools and libraries across the country. Josh currently resides in the small, midwestern town of Chicago, IL.

Chris "Elio" Eliopoulos (*An Animal That Cooks Its Own Dinner*): Chris is a freelance illustrator and comic artist from Elgin, IL. Please visit his website at www.eliohouse.com

Rich Faber (*Roboy Red*): Rich is an illustrator and co-creator of *Roboy Red*. His comic work includes *Steel*, *Green Lantern*, *Impulse*, *Adventures of Superman* and others for DC along with Quicksilver, X-Men, and Uncanny X-Men for Marvel. His illustration and design clients include NASCAR, USA Networks, WWE, Scholastic, and Cartoon Network. Please visit him at www.richfaber.com.

The Fillbach Brothers (*Back In the Day*): The Fillbach Brothers hail from Butte, Montana. Their creations include *Maxwell Strangewell*, *Roadkill: A Jim Kowalski Adventure*, *Werewolves on the Moon: Versus Vampires*, and *Captain Freebird*. They are the face of the *Star Wars: The Clone Wars* digest books. The Fillbach Brothers currently reside in the living cartoon that is Las Vegas, Nevada, where they also write and draw educational comic books for UNLV.

Rachel Friere (*FCHS: Final(s) Crisis!*): Rachel Freire has been doodling since the age of two. She learned to read from Archie comics, which led to her saying "Egads" alot. She attended high school at Art and Design on 56/57th & 2nd Ave, and often wondered "Did John Romita sit in this chair? Maybe Dick Giordano? Art Spiegelman? Or -gasp- Harvey Fierstein??" Now, when she's not working on *FCHS* with Vito Delsante, she's working at Jim Hanley's Universe with Vito Delsante!

Ray Friesen (*Pirate Penguin vs Ninja Chicken*): Ray Friesen is currently 22 years old, but if you read this in the future he might not be anymore. (if you're reading this in the past, Time Travel High Five!) Ray draws lots of silly things, most of which have penguins in them. That's all you need to know. Read more of his cartoons at www.DontEatAnyBugs.com, or else.

John Gallagher (*Roboy Red*): John is the Harvey Award-nominated creator of *Buzzboy*, co-creator of *Roboy Red* (with Rich Faber) and the upcoming *Zoey and Ketchup* (with daughter Katie) graphic novel series. A self-professed comics "evangelist," John was an Eisner Awards nominating judge, and was co-founder of the literacy advocacy group Kids Love Comics. He currently serves as Senior Director of Entertainment at Starbridge Media Group, overseeing properties like Nascar Comics and the Philadelphia Eagles Kids Club Cartoon.

Chris Giarrusso (*G-Man: Reign of the Robo-Teachers*): Chris is the writer/artist of *G-Man* from Image Comics, the illustrator of *The Amazing Adventures of Nate Banks* book series from Scholastic, and the writer/artist of Mini Marvels from Marvel Comics. You can find him online at www.chrisgcomics.com

Jimmy Gownley (*Amelia Rules at the Library*): Jimmy is creator and cartoonist of the graphic novel series, *Amelia Rules!* The books have been translated into multiple languages, are part of Scholastic Book Clubs and Fairs, and were even turned into a stage musical! The newest title, *Amelia Rules: The Tweenage Guide To Not Being Unpopular* hit stores in April 2010. *Amelia Rules: True Things (Adults Don't Want Kids To Know)* is set for Fall 2010.

Daniel Gutowski (*One Day With Amy*): A guy who fell in love with comic books and drawing when was a child. Today, he is drawing mostly for his passion and sometimes for money. Already had some publications in underground zines and comic book anthologies. Now working on his own graphic novel. His art can be seen on degdeg.deviantart.com.

Steve Horton (*One Giant Step*): Steve has written *Captain Marvel* for DC, *Captain Battle* for Image, and many other comics without a quasi-military rank. He lives in Indiana with his wife, two kids and lazy dog.

Dave Lanphear (*One Giant Step*) of Artmonkeys Studios is genus homo ars tecnicus, and whereas he works daily thanks to opposable thumbs, has relegated the skill of staying upright and is likely to be found dreaming pronate. His reveries are in comic books, on TV and film screens, and at www.coroflot.com/artmonkeys.

Kevin LaPorte (*Light's Speed*): A mental health professional by day and aspiring comic writer at all other times, Kevin is currently writing and lettering a web comic, *The Blind Eye* (www.blindeyecomic.com). Other current comic projects include writing *Clown Town*–a finalist in the 2010 Small Press Idol competition–and co-writing The Apocalypse Boyz web comic.

Michael LaRiccia (*Introduction*): In 2005, Michael received a Xeric grant to self-publish *Black Mane*. He has contributed to several anthologies and self-published *The Death of Black Mane and the Feared Self*, *Satori*, and *DISCO*. He exhibits his comic art throughout the country. Currently a full-time graphic designer, LaRiccia periodically teaches cartooning. www.michaellariccia.com.

Christine Larsen (*Heroes*): Originating from the Pine Barrens of central Jersey, Christine is a freelance Illustrator by trade with a BFA in Illustration & Design from the University of the Arts, Philadelphia. She currently does work for numerous clients, including Zuda Comics, Ape Entertainment, Comixology and Applehead Factory. In fall and spring, you will find her traipsing about the University of the Arts campus, where she teaches Foundation Illustration for freshmen and Sequential Format for juniors.

Irene Y. Lee (*Loopy and the Nose of Misfortune*): Irene was born and raised in Queens, New York. She's an avid gamer, comic book reader and anime artist. After graduating from NYU Fine Arts, she managed to land a job at Marvel in the Production department. You can check out her artwork and coloring tutorials at: http://suzuran.deviantart.com/

Alice Meichi Li (*Judgment of Patrick*): True to her namesake, Alice ponders curiouser things and proceeds to ensnare them within the confines of her canvas. Sometimes she even makes illustrations for publishers, rock stars, and the like. She earned her BFA at School of Visual Arts, and currently lives and works in Brooklyn, NY, with her husband and fellow comic geek, Michael. You can view Alice's portfolio here: http://alicemeichi.com/

Russell Lissau (*Heroes*): By day, Russell Lissau is a mild-mannered newspaper reporter in suburban Chicago. By night, he battles evil writing comic books including *The Batman Strikes!*, *The 29*, and *Shrek*. Never one to shy away from a crowd, Lissau also leads workshops at libraries throughout the Chicago area about writing comics. To learn more, check out www.myspace.com/rlissau.

Johnny Lowe (*One Giant Step*) is a letterer who has worked on comics and graphic novels from several companies including Wildstorm, Boom Studios, Image Comics and Devil's Due. He currently lives in Mississippi.

Brandon Montclare (*Editor*) has been a lifelong fan of comics and employed in some part of the business since he was 12 years old. He's worked as an editor at TokyoPop (*Rising Stars of Manga*) and DC Comics (*All Star Superman*, *Batman: Year 100*, *Hellblazer*). And nowadays he's started to write some odds and ends (*Batman*, *Hulk*).

Michael Moreci (*The Replacement Heroes*): Michael Moreci's debut graphic novel, *Quarantined*, will be released with Insomnia publications in 2010. His shorter comics work has appeared (or is forthcoming) in *FutureQuake*, *Something Wicked*, Accent UK's *Victoriana* anthology, and Insomnia's *Layer Zero: Survival* anthology. His freelance journalism has been published in *Wired*, *The Huffington Post*, *North Shore Magazine*, and *In These Times*. Michael lives in Chicago with his wife and dog. Visit him at www.michaelmoreci.com.

Trevor Mueller (*Albert the Alien*): Trevor works in advertising by day, and writes comics by night. He is the creator of several multi-award nominated webcomic series which are self-published. His work can be found on www.trevoramueller.com. In 2009 Trevor joined Reading With Pictures as their Marketing Director, combining his love of comics, education, and advertising. Trevor has also gives lectures and presentations throughout the country at conventions on the power of creativity and literacy.

Tintin Pantoja (*High Noon at Junior High*) was born in Manila and received a BFA in Illustration and Cartooning at the School of Visual Arts in New York, leading to a career in comics and commercial illustration. In 2005 she was nominated for the Friends of Lulu 'Best Newcomer' award and her published works include *Hamlet: The Manga Edition* for Wiley and three volumes of *Manga Math* for Graphic Universe. Check out her art at http://www.tintinpantoja.com

Jay Piscopo (*The Goblin of the Deep*): Jay Piscopo is the author and illustrator of *The Undersea Adventures of Capt'n Eli* all-ages graphic novel series. Piscopo also co-created The Scrap City Pack Rats, art directed the award-winning *Fizz and Martina Math Adventures*, and was an animator for ABC TV's *Squigglevision*. He resides in his hometown of Portland, Maine. www.captneli.com

Phillip Pittz (*A Misguided Field Guide*): Phillip is a specialist in Early Childhood Education with a three decade career as teacher, storyteller, puppeteer and now comics artist/writer. He is the Director of English at his own school in Japan and has begun work on a new series of audio books based on children's literature available through the Gutenberg Project. Phillip can relate with *Lil' Bigfoot* (lilbigfoot.com). He too is messy, smelly and breaks things by accident.

David Precht (*Visual Cues*): David grew up near Chicago and now lives in Seoul with his wife, Lindsay McComb. He loves to cook, write and research, and can grill a mean buffalo burger (the key is goat cheese). He is a blogger and contributor for Soulpancake.com. He is currently working on a graphic novel/webcomic, set in Korea, called *Han* 恨. David can be found at www.davidprecht.com.

Kevin C. Pyle (*The Order of the Secret Pencil*): Kevin is the author/illustrator of the graphic novels *Blindspot* and *Katman*, both published by Henry Holt for Young Readers. *Blindspot* was included in the Best American Comics for 2008, edited by Linda Barry, and Katman was named a Great Graphic Novel for Teens by the Young Adult Library Services Association. Kevin serves as co-editor of the comics anthology World War 3 Illustrated and is also the author/illustrator of several non-fiction "docu-comics." He can currently be found online at http://boatfire.blogspot.com.

Amanda Rachels (*Light's Speed*): Amanda began self-publishing her comic art at the tender age of 17 and never stopped drawing since. She is currently providing full art and colors for a web comic, *The Blind Eye* (www.blindeyecomic.com), and for *Clown Town* - a finalist in the 2010 Small Press Idol Competition.

Grace Randolph (*High Noon at Junior High*) has written for Marvel, DC Comics, Boom! Studios and TOKYOPOP. She also created and hosts the popular web show "Beyond The Trailer." Check out www.gracerandolph.com for more info!

David Reddick (*Legend of Billy*): David is a professional cartoonist and creator of the comic strips Legend of Bill at www.LegendofBill.com, *The Trek Life* for CBS/StarTrek.com, *Gene's Journal* and *Rod & Barry* at Roddenberry.com, and is a staff writer and artist at Paws, Inc., the *Garfield* studio, and was an award-winning staff editorial cartoonist at a daily newspaper for 6 years. Some of David's clients have included Nickelodeon, The New York Times Upfront, IDW Publishing, Image, TOKYOPOP, Paramount Pictures and ROK Media.

Kevin Sacco (*The Order of the Secret Pencil*): Kevin Sacco went to Camberwell Art School in London. After which he came to New York and pursued a career as a storyboard artist for advertising agencies. Along the way he's done some cartoon illustration for *Cracked, Crazy, Scholastic* and *Nuts*. He lives with his wife, son, and daughter in Bloomfield, NJ. More of his work can be seen at http://www.saccoinmontclair.com..

Scott Christian Sava (*The Dreamland Chronicles*) is the award winning creator of *The Dreamland Chronicles, Pet Robots, Hyperactive*, and over a dozen other beloved kids comics enjoyed worldwide. Growing up on *Looney Tunes, Speed Racer, Three Stooges*, and *Spider-Man* has permanently warped Scott's brain to that of a thirteen year old. It's tragic.

Andy Scordellis (*The Replacement Heroes*): Andy always wanted to be an artist, and despite going to Wimbledon Art College, still went on to become a restaurateur for over 20 years. Selling up he moved to Norfolk with his family, and has finally gone back to the drawing board! He contributes regularly to *Futurequake*, and the imminent *Replacement Heroes* series.

Tim Smith 3 (*Loopy and the Nose of Misfortune, Mail Order Ninja*): Tim Smith 3 has done professional work for numerous high-profile entertainment companies over the years. Some of his more recent professional projects include *Spider-Man Unlimited* from Marvel Comics, *Sonic X* from Archie Comics, *Grim & Co.*, an original graphic novel from TokyoPop, *Tales from the Crypt* for Papercutz, and *Teen Titans Go* for DC Comics. Plus many more. To view more of TS3's work, please visit: www.timsmith3.com.

Ian Sokoliwski (*One Giant Step*) is a Canadian colorist, illustrator, and gothic photographer, working professionally in the comic book industry since 1997.

Raina Telgemeier (*A Conversation I Had While Teaching a Comics Class*): Raina Telgemeier is the creator of *SMILE* (Scholastic/Graphix), the adaptor and illustrator of the *Baby-Sitters Club* graphic novel series (Scholastic/Graphix), and the co-author of *X-Men: Misfits* (Del Rey Manga). Raina's comics have been nominated for the Ignatz, Cybil, and Eisner Awards, and have appeared in publications by Random House, DC Comics, *OWL Magazine*, and *Nickelodeon Magazine*. A graduate of Manhattan's School of Visual Arts, Raina currently resides in Astoria, NY. Visit her online at www.goRaina.com.

Jill Thompson (*Cover Artist*): Jill Thompson has been drawing comics for as long as she can remember. Thank goodness she got good at it. She is the creator of *Scary Godmother* and *Magic Trixie*. Follow her on Twitter as @thejillthompson.

Fred Van Lente (*Comics & the Classroom: A Match Made in History*): Fred is the *New York Times* bestselling author of *Incredible Hercules* (with Greg Pak) and *Marvel Zombies 3 & 4*, as well as the American Library Association award-winning *Action Philosophers*. His other comics include *Comic Book Comics, Iron Man Legacy, X Men Noir* and *Amazing Spider-Man*.

Rob Valois (*Editor*) is a senior editor at Penguin Young Readers Group in its Grosset and Dunlap/Price Stern Sloan imprints. He is the editor of the kids' graphic novel series *The Adventures of Daniel Boom aka Loud Boy* as well as the comics-influenced middle-grade series *Splurch Academy for Disruptive Boys*.

Jim Vargas (*Just James*) is a professional colorist and recent recipient of a Bachelors of Fine Arts in Illustration degree from the American Academy of Art. His colorist credits include the webcomics *Divis Morte, Grind House, Dr Leer, No Gods* six cover panoramic illustration, and his own online comic series *Faithless*. www.jimvargas.com

Steve Wallace (*One Day With Amy, Just James, Mail Order Ninja, Pandora*): Steve Wallace is a writer/illustrator/letterer living in Little Rock, Ar. He spends most of his day in front of a computer, the other part he spends in front of a drawing table. You can read his mini-comics and get updates on his upcoming graphic novels at stevewallaceart.com.

Eric Wight (*Frankie Pickle: The Beast that Snored*): Long before he created the *Frankie Pickle* series, Eric Wight spent his childhood wishing for superpowers. When that didn't pan out, he decided to learn how to write and draw. Now he gets to work in his pajamas, and play make-believe for a living. Sometimes nice folks even give him awards for it. Check out all the fun he's having at ericwight.com!

Sari Wilson (Editor) is a former editor at Holt McDougal and currently a Teaching Artist for Teachers & Writers Collaborative in New York City. She's given professional development workshops at Teachers & Writers and the New York City Department of Library Services on incorporating graphic novels into the curriculum. She is an editor with First Second's Drawing Words & Writing Pictures website, for which she served as an educational consultant.

Dave Windett (*Overdue*): Dave is a freelance illustrator and comics artist. His work has been published in Britain, Europe and America. He has worked on comics featuring well-known licensed characters such as *Inspector Gadget, Eek the Cat, Ace Ventura* and *Daffy Duck*. He has also designed original characters for a variety of publications and provided illustrations for everything from magazines and websites to mobile phones, games, and children's shoes. Samples of his work can be seen at www.davewindett.com.

Tory Woollcott (*So Much More*): Tory Woollcott Is a Canadian writer and artist based in Toronto. Her first graphic novel, *Mirror Mind*, recounts her experiences growing up with dyslexia. She is now a graduate from the University of Toronto with an Honors BA, in archeology and near eastern studies. and is currently working on her next book. www.mirrormind.ca

Jeong Mo Yang (*One Giant Step*) was born in S. Korea, then moved to Argentina at age seven and then to the U.S. at fifteen. A human being who loves every type of art form, he believes that art is the ultimate universal language. Art has the power to move hearts and minds, and your heart and mind is no exception. You can check Jeong Mo Yang's artwork at www.comiking.com

Camilla Zhang (Editor, *Loopy and the Nose of Misfortune*): Camilla graduated from Barnard College in 2007 with a BA in English Literature and a Concentration in Creative Writing. As a native New Yorker hailing from the multi-cultural borough of Queens, her greatest passion is writing stories that help her and others have a better understanding of people and of the world. Currently she works at Marvel Entertainment and has an avid devotion to comics as a medium for education and provocative literature.